WOMEN OF CUBA

WOMEN ᵒꜰ CUBA

Inger Holt-Seeland

Translated from the Spanish
by Elizabeth Hamilton Lacoste
with Mirtha Quintanales
and Jose Vigo

With photographs by
Jørgen Schytte

LAWRENCE HILL & CO., INC.
Westport, Connecticut

Copyright © 1981 Inger Holt-Seeland
English translation © 1982 Lawrence Hill & Co., Inc.
All rights reserved

Library of Congress Cataloging in Publication Data:

Holt-Seeland, Inger.
  Women of Cuba.

  Translation of: Con las puertas abiertas.
  Includes bibliographical references.
  1. Women—Cuba. 2. Women—Cuba—Case studies.
3. Women's rights—Cuba. I. Title.
HQ1508.H6413   305.4′2′097291   82-2889
ISBN 0-88208-142-X   AACR2
ISBN 0-88208-143-8 (pbk.)

First English-language edition published 1982 by
Lawrence Hill & Co., Inc., 520 Riverside Avenue,
Westport, Connecticut 06880

1 2 3 4 5 6 7 8 9

Design by Sandra Kopell
Printed in the United States of America

CONTENTS

TO THE READER

In 1946 I left Norway on a pilgrimage to Europe and the two Americas. I visited Cuba for the first time in 1949, but it wasn't until 1959 that my stay became more permanent.

In Cuba I worked as an assistant director in the cinema, as a producer for theater and television, and as a foreign newspaper correspondent. I had children and I wrote this book on Cuban women. The following pages are few, and the objective is modest— to highlight what characterizes Cuban women at different stages of life; their culture; what they bring to Cuban life; and their transcendant social responsibility.

It is a book to which more could be added every day. Its news value is short-lived. For Cuba is at the vortex of a movement that changes without tiring, and women's equality is given high priority by a government that aspires to build a "new society" within a self-proclaimed Marxist-Leninist revolution.

It is an enormous task for Cuban women to eradicate the effects of centuries of backwardness within the framework of a political process that is not free from error. Will Cuban women win complete political, social and economic freedom? The doors stand open!

MY THANKS

To the Cuban Women's Federation and the National
Association of Small Farmers, who gave me their support
To all those who in some way encouraged me
To Elena, for sharing her heart.

WOMEN OF CUBA

1

*"...the campaigns of the people
are weak only if   lo not
engage the woman's heart..."*

—JOSÉ MARTÍ

ELENA/Farmworker

The agricultural cooperative Celso Maragoto is located a little over two hundred kilometers from Havana, the capital of the Republic of Cuba, in Pinar del Rio, the island's westernmost province. The cooperative was formed in September 1977, after Prime Minister Fidel Castro discussed, during the Fifth Congress of the National Associationof Small Farmers (ANAP, Asociación Nacional de Agricultores Pequeños), the need to implement new forms of agricultural production.

The cooperative has a membership of ninety-four persons, forty-five of whom are women. With fifty scattered houses, it comprises 190 hectares of rich soil given over mainly to the cultivation of tobacco—considered the best in the world. Other crops include peppers, for export, and rice, beans, tubers, and vegetables for domestic consumption throughout the island and among members of the cooperative.

It has been established that it was in Cuba that the white man first saw tobacco used. In his log for Tuesday, November 6, 1492, Christopher Columbus wrote about the *bohío* (the traditional peasant dwelling on the island) and tobacco: "two travelers encountered many men and women going from town to town carrying a burning wand in their hands...aromatic herbs they were accustomed to using...."

THE BOHÍO

Elena's house is a typical Cuban bohío. Its walls are built of palm wood; the thatched roof is constructed of adroitly intertwined palm-tree leaves supported by sturdy wooden planks. The living room-dining area, the kitchen, and two bedrooms have low dividing walls. Curtains hang where there would be doors, providing little privacy but allowing the air to circulate and cool the interior of the bohío. The kitchen opens into a spacious backyard where one can see the laundry tub under the shade of a tree. Somewhat at a distance, among the high grasses at the edge of an old fence, one finds the *excusado*, the outhouse, built of unpainted rough-hewn wooden planks.

Only the front of the bohío is freshly painted, light blue. The rest of the building remains weather-beaten. This is typical, however, a custom found not only in the countryside but in towns and cities as well. When it is impossible to paint the exterior of an entire building, the front, considered the most important, is given priority. The rest can wait, if necessary.

Beyond the bohío's front porch, with its two massive rocking chairs, there is a garden full of roses and a variety of other flowers. On each side of the bohío is a narrow path laced with white periwinkle, which is used to make an eyewash.

In the backyard, a lively chorus of ducks, turkeys, and hens wander among mango, coconut, orange, and lemon trees.

Small, slim, with timid eyes and short, wavy hair falling across her brow, Elena is serving coffee in the small foyer where the management of the cooperative is gathered. The aromatic nectar is served black and sweet, as is the custom throughout the island.

The wooden furniture is old but sports new, brightly-colored slip covers; the usual vase of artificial flowers rests on a small coffee table. On top of a Soviet television set there is a rubber doll dressed in a bridal gown. Wall shelves are filled with paper flowers and figurines of plaster and plastic. The polished cement floor is immaculately clean despite the traipsing about of chickens that nobody seems to notice.

The conversation turns to the cooperative and tobacco. Women begin to arrive. There are five of them in the cooperative's management, which is composed of thirteen members.

"At present, the advance is given to all members of the cooperative regardless of sex or occupation. This first year it's a small sum so that we won't go into debt; we've already bought two tractors."

They explain that at year's end a settlement is made with them on the basis of the cooperative's profits, minus the advance.

"Next year wage standards will be established. Produce will be paid for by the box, and the planting of seedlings by the thousand. The spraying of crops, a hazardous job, will be better paid; even with precautions it can affect one's health..." "Women cannot spray crops, it is harmful to their reproductive system."

"The hardest chores are done by the men who work between eight and ten hours a day...and, additionally, take turns watering the crops and the rice at night."

"Every once in a while, when there are no suitable jobs for women, they go several days without work."

"In the old days—before the Revolution—our women had no choice but to do men's work...the rent had to be paid to the latifundist; but when the Revolution gave the land to those who worked it in 1962, women stopped doing rough chores, except in unusual cases."

"Tomorrow we're going to pick peppers. That's a job for women only."

"And the men, what are they doing tomorrow?"

"They're planting rice. That's awful work...There isn't a woman here who would do it...Of course, we were forced to do it many times in the past, when we had no choice—but today!"

Pablo, a tall, strong, older black man who is responsible for production, adds with great seriousness: "We take into consideration that the women have already been through enough hardship, and we don't see any reason why our daughters and granddaughters should have to continue suffering."

"How do you feel about equality between the sexes?"

"It's not that I consider women inferior and so must protect them. Let's say instead...that I consider them delicate and that they must be looked after."

The men laugh and applaud his comment. Pastora, his wife, big and strong like her husband, stares at him askance, telling him: "Remember that when it's time to feed the pigs."

Pastora is the organizer of the cooperative but she cannot continue in the position unless she begins to study, as she has a poor education.

Twenty-two women and men are attending sixth grade and high school Monday through Friday evenings. Others are pursuing their studies on their own and attending classes only on Saturday during the day.

The lack of a daycare center for children is one of the most pressing problems for the women of the cooperative. As yet, there is no solution.

"Why not agree among yourselves to take turns caring for the children?"

"The conditions in the bohíos are not suitable for caring for them well and it would be a great burden. When the new buildings are constructed, there will be a daycare center. We figure that with two more harvests as good as this year's we will be able to request a loan from the bank to begin to build our new community, which will also have a school, a cafeteria, a beauty parlor, and a commercial center. The work there will be principally for women."

(The cooperative's objectives have subsequently been delayed by an epidemic of "blue mold" that attacked tobacco and destroyed the 1980 crop. This unexpected setback, however, has been compensated by an unprecedented success in the production of black beans and other crops).

"Do you prefer apartments to individual homes?"

"We don't prefer them," Elena interrupts, "but like Fidel said, population increases as land decreases. We have to conserve land, we need it for farming. Apartment buildings are also much more economical for the state, which finances them. They are more economical for us too, because we want to get out of debt as soon as possible. There are many other cooperatives that we must help."

Until now Elena has not spoken. Here, however, among the many people at the meeting, she has expressed herself with great fluency.

A neighbor adds that Elena soaks things up like a sponge. She finished high school with excellent grades, but then got pregnant, had her first daughter and since she didn't have anyone to babysit for her, she decided to study Russian. Now she continues her studies through television.

"Do you know why she chose Russian?"

"Because she could study it at home. René, her husband, studied in the Soviet Union on a scholarship before they were getting married, and he speaks the language rather well. He helps her study."

WHAT IS A WOMAN WITHOUT A MAN?

René, a highly specialized mechanic, is not a member of the cooperative. He works far away from home and returns only on weekends. In his absence, Nene, Elena's brother and president of the cooperative, "represents" her. It is still important for the majority of Cuban women to have a man speak for them.

The topic at hand is discussed, and one of the women says, blushing: "But what is a woman without a man?" Another woman joins in: "And what is a man without a woman? Have you seen an unhappier person than the man who's used to having a woman around when he's left alone?" Still another adds: "Mine doesn't even light the fire to heat his food the few times I go out. Imagine that! When I was in the hospital for fifteen days he didn't eat except when the neighbors invited him over. And as far as I know, he's not an exceptional case."

"Do they help at home? Do they follow the Family Code?"

Pastora jumps to her feet and explains that the men of Celso Maragoto work more than eight hours a day and that the women seldom work more than a half day's shift, that "it wouldn't be fair to expect them to comply with the Code's regulations on sharing housework. We can't apply the rules mechanically," she concludes, gesturing with her coarse but manicured hands; her long fingernails are brightly painted like those of most Cuban women.

"From now on," a young woman interrupts, "they should help out more so that they get used to it when we women have to work the whole day."

"Well, they always help with something," another woman re-
plies. "What's bad is that it doesn't go beyond that. We have to thank
them for helping us as if it were a favor, while it continues to be an
obligation for the women."

"Then there hasn't been any change."

"Of course, there has! There's been a very important change,"
Elena interjects. "A change of attitude toward women. If men don't
help, at least they recognize that they ought to and excuse themselves. They say they aren't used to it, that they don't know how to
do those things. They have become aware of the historic discrimination and exploitation of women by men. And this includes men who
today consider themselves revolutionaries, some of whom fall back
on the convenience afforded by tradition...this isn't fair. I think
today's men are struggling with themselves, wavering between convenience and conscience. Before, they weren't aware that they were
exploiters of women or that they were being exploited by the latifundists.
Anyone who had power abused it: this was considered his preroga-
tive. Since women were weaker, it was natural that men should ex-
ploit them, right?"

A woman in her forties, pretty in spite of some missing teeth,
breaks in with a grin: "No man in the cooperative would think of
forbidding his wife to work or study. Look, my husband came to me
one day when the cooperative started to tell me he had signed me up
as a member. That was the happiest day of my life!"

"He didn't ask you first whether you wanted to join?"

"No. He knew very well that I've always wanted to work outside
the home. Why should he have asked? Besides, he's used to making
decisions on his own. I don't recall his ever having consulted me on
anything."

She talks about getting her teeth fixed. "I'm getting them done
at the polyclinic in town," she says with great satisfaction.

She is a mother of five. The oldest, seventeen years old, is also a
member of the cooperative; her anxious and distrustful glances attract
our attention.

"MY DAUGHTER IS PREGNANT, SHE'S BEEN DISGRACED . . ."[1]*

Elena tells us that Amalí's oldest daughter was "disgraced" by her cousin and that people had found out about it through the young man's indiscretion.

"They've bad luck with their daughters," she continues. "The other one, only fourteen years old, got pregnant by a local boy. He took her home to live with him when he returned from military service and—wouldn't you know it—as soon as he found a good job in a machine shop he sent her home because she was 'boring' him. Her father has tried to convince him to do 'his duty' by her, at least until the child is born, but he refuses. Now, he's going to have to do it anyway, because the law protects her. She's a minor." Elena tells us that she herself would never marry off one of her daughters under those circumstances, "but the girl's father says he doesn't care. What he wants is his daughter to be left a divorced woman, not an unwed mother. Having another child in the house where there is barely room for the others does not bother him, nor does it bother him to have to play the role of father to his grandson."

Elena also feels that since Cubans like children, whether their own or someone else's, "this won't be an obstacle to the girl marrying some other man in the future, although it's doubtful that it would be someone from this area who'd know her misfortune."

"You mean to say that she'd have to lie to her future husband about how the child—"

"No, I don't mean to say that." Elena denies it, waving her hands. "In any case, the truth will be known sooner or later, but it is a different thing to *hear* the story than to see her live through the shame in front of people. Sometimes I start to think, Why is it that the shame always falls on the one who shows the belly and not on the one who caused it?"

"According to what you say, there is no sexual equality."

"No. At least not here in the countryside. A man suffers no loss of reputation by running around with women, while it only takes one

*Notes will be found on pages 107-9.

man to disgrace a woman. What's more, a man is expected to have his 'experiences' before he gets married since he's the one who's supposed to teach his women about those things, and . . . if he has his escapades afterwards, nobody questions it. But a woman has to be careful because, in that case, not only does she look bad, but her husband is ridiculed."

"Do you think that's fair?"

"Perhaps it isn't. But it is a difficult custom to change. In spite of that there have been great improvements. Just think how badly divorced women were viewed before! That's no longer the case. They remarry in the blink of an eye, and it often seems they're more sought after than single women. It's true, a woman who has not married by the time she's thirty will have a lot of difficulty doing so. People around here begin to think right away that something's wrong with her.

"Nowadays women don't stand for even a quarter of what they used to have to take from men. Ask around. You'll see that it's almost always the woman who asks for a divorce, especially among the new generation."

BREAKING WITH OLD TRADITIONS

Following peasant tradition, Elena had shut the bohío tight at bedtime. During the night, the heat inside was unbearable. A dim lightbulb hanging from the eaves was left burning until the early morning.

As dawn arrives, a pleasant coolness sweeps over the fields. The roosters crow, and the sound of the first tractors can be heard.

Elena complains about the heat, but admits she is afraid to sleep with the windows open. She can't pinpoint the source of her fears; there are no thieves or dangerous animals in the area.

"I think I'm just afraid of breaking lifelong habits," she says pensively. "But let's open one window. After all, in this Revolution we have had to break with even more deeply rooted traditions."

She promises to turn off the outside light from now on, but she insists on keeping one on in her bedroom. She will continue to close the rest of the windows, "getting used to the change little by little."

During the slow season Elena, like most of the women in the cooperative, gets up between six and seven in the morning. By that time the men are already on their way to the rice fields. She opens up the house and takes down and gathers the mosquito nets, which do not appear again until nighttime "because they look ugly and unkempt." The peasant woman who doesn't put the mosquito nets away before mid-morning is considered a poor housewife.

"A thin white cloth moved gently by the breeze, what is ugly about that?"

"Well, if you put it that way...I don't know. But we're used to viewing it as a sign of neglect. And besides, you wouldn't be able to see the bedspread.

"Traditions are strange, aren't they?" she continues. "If you learn to see something as ugly, you'll keep thinking it's ugly until you find out that perhaps it isn't. Then you begin, for the first time, to look at it with no other thought than trying to decide for yourself whether you really like it or not." With a worried expression she walks away to prepare breakfast.

Her children drink a cold glass of milk while standing and hastily eat a large piece of buttered bread before leaving for school.

As Elena is feeding the chickens the neighbor's hog, which has been rooting in her garden, rushes in, frightens them away, and eats their food. Elena doesn't seem to pay much attention.

"Doesn't it bother you?"

"What can you do?" she says, shrugging her shoulders. "This is one of the problems of cooperative living. If I had a hog, I'm sure it would also bother my neighbor. In the country we just learn to tolerate each other and not get annoyed by minor things." She explains that soon all the animals—cows, hogs, sheep, and fowl—will be rounded up for the benefit of the members of the cooperative.

"We're going to build corrals for them and assign women to their care. We're doing this not only to keep the animals from going into everybody's yards but for other reasons as well. One of them is to end the kind of thinking that says, 'This is my cow, and so I'm going to give the milk to my hogs,' instead of making it available to a neighbor who might need it for a child or an elderly relative. Besides, when we move to the new cooperative buildings, we won't be able to have animals running through hallways, we are all agreed about this. Also, we will receive payment for them in the same way that we are receiving payment for the value of the land and the tools that we contributed when we joined the cooperative. This means an amount equivalent to what each member originally brought to the cooperative."

Elena puts black beans, which she had left soaking the night before, "to soften them," on the stove. We head off toward the tobacco barn, where several work crews of women have begun the daily tasks of processing the tobacco.

THE TOBACCO BARN

A scant three hundred meters separate Elena's bohío from the tobacco barn. As we walk there, she explains briefly how the leaf is handled before it is sold to the factories. "During this period we 'strip' the tobacco every morning while it is still 'soft.' "

The Cuban scholar Fernando Ortiz, in his book *Contrapunteo Cubano del Tabaco y el Azúcar* (Cuban counterpoint: Tobacco and sugar), writes: "From the time it sprouts, tobacco is already tobacco in essence. That is why the Spaniards adopted the Indian word: . . . It is tobacco in the seedbed, on the leaf, in its manufacture, and at the moment it is consumed in ashes and clouds of smoke."

After it is picked fresh from the fields, the tobacco is strung together by women using a large needle and a long thread, which is then tied to the two ends of a long and flexible stick. Forked poles running from ceiling to floor hold the sticks horizontally, so that the leaves can dry. The "untying" begins when the tobacco has dried and consists of lowering the sticks, plucking the leaves, tying them in sheafs of approximately fifty leaves and turning them into bunches of four sheafs tied together. This is a small part of a very long process.

When you enter the redolent barn from the blinding brightness of morning, your eyes must readjust to the half darkness within. The sun, filtering in through thin cracks in the boards in the walls and flooding in through the many shutters, gradually loses its intensity until it is caught by the barriers formed by the thousands of sticks hanging in the large rooms containing millions of smooth, fragrant leaves covered with soft fuzz.

The happy voices of chatting women are lowered as they greet us, only to rise again as they go about their work again. Their able hands strip the sticks and turn the leaves into bunches that pile up in the center of the barn. The leaves are handled while still pliable from the dampness that night brings, making them less susceptible to cracking and splitting. From then on, the job of making the hundred-pound packages bound with palm bark is "man's work." It is also man's work to climb up on the beams of the barn to bring down the sticks.

"If you always give the men the hardest work, doesn't that restrict you when it comes time to demand equal rights?"

"Sometimes we also climb up there, but not usually. Men are always given the heaviest jobs, but that doesn't mean they are in charge. The head of the brigade is Elda, and the compañeros obey her.

"We have four old, retired men who still want to help," Elena explains. "They can do packing and other jobs that are not too heavy. Look at Chiquitico"—she points to a short, muscular man in his thirties— "the one up there on the crosswalk. He has diabetes. When he was a farmer, he did all his own chores. We don't allow him to do all that here. We give him work that won't aggravate his condition."

Elena suddenly remembers she's left the beans on the stove. She leaves for the bohío in a hurry. She must cook lunch before she goes to pick peppers with her brigade in the afternoon.

Without stopping work, the women begin a lively discussion of the changes they would demand before getting involved with the men in the hardest chores.

Chiquitico up above begins to laugh so hard he has to hold on to something to steady himself. An elderly man grumbles as he tightens the band around a pack of leaves: "Who would have believed it? That things would come to this? Women have no respect anymore." No one listens to his protest.

ELDA/Brigade Leader

Elda, twenty years old, is a member of Communist Youth, a high school student, and has studied accounting. She tells us that she recently received a good job offer in the city, twelve kilometers from home. Nene asked her not to accept it since he was counting on her to keep the cooperative's books "as soon as the harvest begins." She agreed to wait a few months before beginning her new job at the cooperative where she'll earn a little less than at the job she was offered in the city.

"So why did you accept?"

"Because I like it here. I grew up here. I've been in the cooperative since it was founded. So have my father and my brothers... Well, I guess you could say my whole family... In this place everyone is related to everyone else in one way or another, and those who are not treat each other as if they were." Then, lowering her voice, "I also don't believe that the youth of the countryside should move to the cities... except in cases where it's necessary... not me! No way!... If I've got a job here, why should I leave for a few extra pesos?"

"Isn't it boring for young people to live far away from the attractions of the city?"

"Not at all. That was before the Revolution, when the only diversion in this area was the cockfights. Men would gamble away their children's food money and often the whole thing would end up in a machete fight. What a shame! Now we have open-air movies, several nearby beaches where we go in groups to bathe, fish, or hunt for crabs. There are dances and gatherings in the Social Club or in nearby cooperatives. And we can get there in a wagon drawn by the tractors. And what a good time we have! We have a budget for gas, musicians, salaries, and other such things. People visit each other a lot around here. They slaughter hogs on Sundays and without an invitation to anyone—it's not necessary, believe me—people come and eat, drink beer, and enjoy the *décimas*[2] that people improvise. No, we don't have time to be bored, and I haven't even told you about night school, Federation or Committee meetings. And although communal meetings are not entertainment, they keep us from getting bored."

"Do you have a boy friend?"

"No." She blushes. "I don't have one."

"Come on, now. So pretty, and no boy friend? Aren't there any single men around here?"

"Yes, of course there are"—hiding her smile with her hands—"yes, yes, there are."

By the way she repeats it and the gleam in her eyes, it's obvious that she is thinking of someone in particular.

We return to the topic of tobacco. The women are proud of the harvests and of the quality of the leaf. They have me feel the leaves, smell them, admire their color, size, and smoothness; tobacco has been a part of their lives from birth. Only now, with the creation of the Cooperative, it has gained a new significance. It has come to mean stable working conditions, the right to share profits, maternity leave, retirement, and other benefits.

It's ten o'clock, and getting warmer. The leaves are losing their suppleness. Before the women disperse and return to their bohíos to prepare lunch, I receive invitations to their homes, meet their families, and eat with them. Some of them mention slaughtering hogs, turkeys, or hens to celebrate my visit. In vain, I explain that I prefer to try their everyday meals.

EVEN GOOD THINGS TAKE GETTING USED TO

We meet Elena again in the yard under the trees by the laundry. She is carrying water in pails that she fills from the tap near the kitchen. A few meters away, on a fire built over stones, white clothing is being boiled in a large, blackened tin can. Energetically, she scrubs at the clothes with a brush.

"Doesn't the washing machine work?"

"Yes," she answers, a bit surprised by the question. "It's just that I almost always forget. We bought it only recently. When I have little to wash, like today, it seems easier to wash it by hand." She shakes her head. "Even the good things take getting used to."

"Let's go to the kitchen and have a cup of coffee," she says, drying her hands on the towel tied round her waist.

A kerosene fire is burning on the stove. "For lunch we're having *congrí* (rice and black beans), pork, *yuca con mojo* (manioc with olive oil and garlic), and tomato salad. Ah! and for dessert, grated coconut with fresh cheese," she says proudly. She explains that in Cuba they eat two hot meals a day, and that if there aren't any rice and beans, most people feel they haven't eaten.

As if attracted by the aroma of fresh-brewed coffee, two young friends of Elena arrive, Matilde, robust and smiling, and Dania, her sister-in-law, petite and delicate. They tell us, among other things, that they built their houses all by themselves, a fact that piques our interest, and so we decide to visit them.

WE WORKED SO HARD!

They are not from around here, but from a place eight kilometers closer to the city. Childhood friends, they married two brothers and went to live at their mother-in-law's house. The house was located in an area that today is part of the Cooperative. When the mother-in-law sold her land to the cooperative, she went to work as a cook in the canteen of a food canning factory. Matilde and Dania, on the other hand, became members of the Celso Maragoto Cooperative, where they work very enthusiastically. Their husbands, who are truck drivers, work at a nearby quarry.

Despite the fact that they love their mother-in-law, they lost no time in deciding to build their own homes. They had little money, and their husbands had too many other responsibilities to help. So the women undertook the construction of the houses themselves, despite the many difficulties and a scarcity of materials. "And we did it in spite of hell and high water," says Matilde.

"In the beginning," Dania says, "people laughed at us. But when they saw us put up the walls, they began to respect us, and some folks even gave us a hand. Our husbands only helped us on Sundays since they go to the farm workers' night school."

Both houses are built out of concrete blocks, and Dania used one of the walls of her mother-in-law's house as a support. Between her house and Matilde's there is a four-meter space where Matilde's eight-year-old daughter and Dania's six-year-old son are playing.

"How old are you?" I ask the women. "You look very young."

"Matilde is twenty-six and I'm twenty-four."

The houses are somewhat narrow and elongated, and the concrete blocks of the outside walls have not been stuccoed. Each house has a living room-dining area, a kitchen, a bathroom, and two bedrooms. The interiors are finished and painted in bright colors. The roofs are part zinc, part prefabricated material. "We grabbed whatever we could get our hands on. We had to be inventive. When we ran out of cinder-blocks, we made them ourselves from a mix."

It is a job that took strength, courage, and ingenuity. Their inventiveness is admirable. Everything is made from scraps; a few things were bought, some were donated, and much was improvised. They have toilets, and even though they haven't found water tanks for them, they work fine—"if you throw in a bucketful of water."

"We've worked so hard! It's going to be a shame to move in to the new community when it's built. We'll be among the first to get an apartment since the buildings will be constructed right around where we live."

"Why here?"

"In part because it's closer to the highway, but also because the land is not as fertile as it is down there"—Dania points with her fingers—"next to the marsh where Elena lives."

I'VE SEEN THE ANIMALS DOING IT

"More children?" they inquire in unison. "Wouldn't dream of it." And Matilde argues that modern life is too demanding to raise more than one or two children well.

"We want to start night school next term, and since we do chores around the the house and work in the cooperative, we also like to have a good time, go to the beach. We're young, you know! With one child you can manage, but with several you become a slave. Besides, the country doesn't need more kids, anyway," she finishes triumphantly.

"What measures do you take to prevent pregnancy?"

"Well, most of us young married women use the I.U.D. The older ones keep having babies until they have their tubes tied or until the doctor at the polyclinic convinces them to use the I.U.D. Abortion is also utilized."

"What did your mother teach you about sex?"

"About—about that, nothing. Well, she mentioned it once when I was eleven or twelve so I wouldn't get scared. All in all, she said it was a curse, something women had to put up with if they wanted to have children. That was it. But I knew something...I'd seen the animals doing it. And what could you expect the old woman to tell me? Poor thing, she was illiterate until the Revolution educated her. Of course, today there are lectures on health at Federation meetings and at the Polyclinic, but even so there is still a lot of ignorance. Did you hear about the fourteen-year-old girl with the belly and the culprit hiding so that he wouldn't have to face up to it? I, Matilde Gonzales, say that there's no worse vermin than men."

"What do you think might be done about such problems?"

"We should learn about these things even if it has to be in school." Turning to Dania, "Why not, Dania? Why should you be embarrassed about, uh, sex. It's only natural. If I had it my way, I'd make everyone take classes on the subject—children, teenagers, even men . . . because you better believe that men don't know any better than we women do. Even if they're way more experienced."

"Do you mean that they have more practice?"

"Yes, they have more practice, but sometimes that doesn't teach them anything. I could tell you some stories." We all laugh.

"And you, Dania? What do you think of men and housework?"

"Well, my husband doesn't help me much, but with working and studying he doesn't have time.

"You won't have time either when you begin to study at night."

"It's true, but since he's so useless, I can't count on him at home."

"And you, Matilde?"

"Our mother-in-law, good as she may be, didn't know how to raise her children. She was left alone with them when her husband was murdered during the Batista era. And she had to take in people's laundry for a pittance. Of course, the boys helped her by gathering firewood in the marsh, tending the animals and other such things. But housework? Never! That was unheard of. She felt sorry for her kids—so young and fatherless. But nobody felt sorry for her, not the children who took everything for granted. I can't complain about Arturo. He's a good man. He devotes all his time to me, and what he earns is for our home, although sometimes I'd like to see him at least pick up his own clothing."

"Give it to me!" "Mommy, tell him to give it to me!" "Let go!" "He wants my toys and boys don't play with girl's toys!" "Boys don't cry! You sissy!"

The noise is deafening. Mothers and children are yelling at each other. Dania says she's getting tired of telling her son not to touch his cousin's toys. He's a young man and she would rather "see him dead than a queer."

SOMETIMES LESS IS BETTER THAN MORE

The sun hangs suspended at the zenith of the sky. A mist rises from the ground. It is cool only inside the bohío.

Elena emerges from the bathhouse next to her house. The zinc roof and the vertical planks of its walls are different from those of the rest of the bohío, revealing that it was built at a later time. Water falls in a fine spray from the sprinkler that hangs from the roof as an improvised shower head. A metal tank above it is heated by the sun. A small hole in the cement floor provides drainage through a pipe that disappears into the ground. The soap rests on the window sill, and through the small window one can see a mirrorlike pond in the distance. A piece of cheesecloth, doubled, serves as a door.

"I feel like a new person! A bath is so refreshing in this heat! You don't need much to feel good. There are a lot of people who want many things because they think they will enjoy life more. They're wrong! Sometimes less is better than more."

"How do you explain that?"

"I believe that when you don't have much, you take pleasure in small things. When you have to struggle to better yourself, you are able to enjoy simple things more. A small flower you find in your garden makes you happy. So does the fact that tomorrow is Sunday or that your children are bringing you a present on Mother's Day."

"Do you mean to say that your sensitivity is somehow purer?"

"Something like that. If you have a lot, you end up feeling that you never have enough, and it isn't possible to be happy living like that. If I need to get a toilet in order to get rid of the outhouse, and if a tank and a bowl will do fine, why pine for a big black marble bathroom filled with mirrors and fancy faucets? But there are many people who can't live without these things or without servants to clean and polish the bathroom tiles. One thing leads to another, and soon they think they need a whole ton of unnecessary things."

A pleasant aroma coming from the kitchen promises a restorative meal. Elena doesn't sit down at the table.[3] Like most peasant women, she never does, not with her family or with guests. "It's just that later I eat more calmly, after I have straightened things out," she excuses herself.

After lunch and a cup of black coffee, we take a short siesta. Resting on the cool grass, under the trees, we wait for the other women to arrive to go pick peppers. With a long, flexible pole, Elena knocks down several coconuts containing fresh, sweet milk. She sings a song that lulls us to sleep.

FIDEL AND THE VIRGIN

The wall of vegetation along the sides of the path is almost impenetrable. Between clearings, the marsh appears—grayish mud, cattails, long and slender ("On the way back from harvesting the peppers I'm going to gather some cattails to make a small pillow for my son," someone says), dainty blue waterlilies floating in the water. Over the voices of the women the birds sing: plowbirds, mockingbirds, hummingbirds. The air is heavy with fragrances, inviting sensuality. What a wonderful place for romance!

We allow a cart drawn by two huge white oxen to pass us. The old driver greets us peevishly, gazing at us through smallish eyes framed by thick, bushy eyebrows. It seems as though he is going to say something, but he continues on his way.

"That damned old man is a Jehovah's Witness," one of the women exclaims. "He's the only one left around here. Always butting in. But nobody pays any attention to him. Religion is dying out with the old people."

"Nevertheless, you can still find religious articles in many homes," I tell the women. "And in yours, Elena, there is a statue of the Virgin in the bedroom. But in the living room there is a picture of Fidel hanging on a wall."

"Compañera, what does Fidel have to do with the Virgin? He's not a fantasy god but a real-life leader. The statue of the Virgin belonged to my grandmother, who spent her entire life praying to the saints to pluck her out of her miserable existence. However, Fidel had to come through with the agrarian reform before the old woman could die knowing that the land she stood on was finally hers. There is no reason for me to throw away the memento just because it happens to be the statue of the Virgin. Now, I am always telling my children that it is plain ignorance, that business of praying to dolls."

"And what do the rest of you think? Are there any believers among you? How about you, with the green bandana?"

"Mercedes Luján, at your service"

"Do you ever pray?"

"Well, I—I don't deny it. I pray sometimes when I have a serious problem. And it's not that I believe, but I don't stop believing either. I tell myself: it's better to pray just in case. Besides, I don't hurt anybody by doing it. I'm a good worker and a "mother in action."* Everyone knows me and could tell you that I never fail in carrying out my tasks for the Revolution."

And what is your religious affiliation: Protestant, Catholic, Jehovah's Witness?"

"God forbid, compañera!" she exclaims, raising her hands to her head. "Don't you know that those Jehovah's Witnesses are a bunch of counterrevolutionaries? Their creed does not allow them to defend their country or to salute the flag. They spend most of their time conspiring against Cuba, and *that* seems to be permitted. Besides, they are so backward that they prefer to watch their children die than give them a blood transfusion. Near the Cooperative there was such a case, and do you know what the neighbors did? They kidnapped the child and took him to the hospital against his parent's will—which was a good thing. If not. . . " Mercedes traces an imaginary line across her neck with her fingers, like a knife cutting a throat. "There is no way I believe in any church! I pray to God and the Virgin, but when I want to and in my own way."

Mercedes' comments generate a great deal of laughter among the women, who seemed to agree with her. "Well, when you think about it, one never knows for sure, and if you feel better praying, why not pray?" None of them considers herself to be deeply religious.

"In Cuba, even the believers forget the gods in heaven and strug-

---

*An honorary title given to certain women in Cuba. (See page 97.)

gle down here on earth when the nation is in danger," Elena concludes, meeting everyone's approval.

Suddenly we come upon a clearing where about twenty men are working, ankle deep in muddy water. Nene comes over to greet us.

"You should come over here and see for yourself that this is not work for women," he says as he steps out of the water onto the firm ground where we are standing.

There is laughter and joking. "Haven't you gained a little weight around the ankles, Tomás?" Still laughing, the women continue on their way.

"Honestly, this isn't work for men either," Nene adds. "But since we don't have enough machines, we need to keep at it. Like Ché said: If we don't have tractors, we'll use oxen."

"Is there any job worse than this one?"

"No way! Can you imagine what it's like? With the hot sun grilling us from above, and the hot mud cooking us from below? Can you imagine a woman with her 'female trouble' working in this hell?"

The workers, each working in his own row, move in a monotonous, slow syncopated dance. At close intervals, rice seedlings, damp with drops of perspiration from tanned faces hidden in the shadows of straw hats, are sprinkled over the muddy water. The workers's feet, alternatively lifted out of the mud and set down again, produce discordant sounds like the sobs of a troubled mother earth.

"Why don't you wear boots?"

"Compañera, it's obvious that in your country people never do this kind of work. You can rest assured that there isn't a being in this world who can walk around in this mess wearing boots."

Manuel, a quixotic figure, improvises a *décima*.

> Deep in the marshes
> Mortals crawl like reptiles.
> The fertile sun rays bear
> Down on them in the swamps
> While the fields
> Murmur nearby.
> They carry peppers in their hands
> Like flower buds.

There is a roar of approval.

Following the women's trail we arrive at another clearing where, beneath the shade of a hundred-year-old silk-cotton tree, there is an earthenware jug containing fresh water.

The muted green of the shrubbery blends with the bright green, red, and orange of the peppers—swollen, fleshy, and firm to the touch. In a large field women hand two men baskets loaded with peppers. The men then empty the baskets into wooden crates with an even rhythm despite the conversation. "If it were cooler, the task would be enjoyable." "They aren't heavy, they're full of air."

Amalí is curious about the lives of peasants in countries where I've lived. The women interrupt their work to ask me questions. They return to their tasks only after I have promised to talk to them tomorrow evening at the meeting of the Federation.

GIVING BIRTH

Amalí talks about her life. Born in the mountains, she was the eldest of eleven children, her parents poor landless coffee growers. Her father had cleared some land on steep terrain near the foot of a hill which, until then, had never been cultivated. The landlord received half of the annual harvest as rent and bought the other half at prices to his advantage. Thus, "year after year we were always in debt. The owner, as was customary in those days, supplied the food, the fertilizer, the work tools, all at exorbitant prices.

"We lived isolated in the hills. I seldom had shoes, and electricity came in only with the Revolution. . . . I was twenty years old. After the victory, my brothers and I learned to read. Now the youngest of them is an engineer and has a Fiat. If mom could only see him! She's passed away. How proud she would be. Poor mother. I'm sure that now she wouldn't have so many children, always fearing that some of them would die at birth. She was as skinny as a rail, worn out by work and poverty. She was forty-two when she died. . . She suffered more than any of us."

"How did she manage when she was giving birth? Who helped her?"

"When she gave birth, a neighbor would assist her. In the countryside all the women knew how to do it. I truly have been lucky. When I gave birth to my last one, I spent a month in the maternity home. Since it was my fifth, I had my tubes tied".

"The maternity home, what is it like?" How does it work?"

"It works very well. I spent the time resting, talking with the other women. The food was good and the doctors were all young. For the first time in my life I knew what it was like to have no responsibilities. But what was most important to me was what I learned from talking to the other women. It's true what they say about ignorance. We talked about everything without fear."

"Like what?"

"I'll try to explain. It isn't easy. I found that the problems I have are almost the same as theirs. My husband never let me have friends, but now, after being a member of the Cooperative, I feel freer. I used to live with the fear that he'd leave me if I didn't please him. Not anymore.

"One day when he was complaining, I told him: If you want to, leave. With what Amalí-María and I earn, and with what you will have to give the children by law, we will have enough. He was speechless, and since then we don't fight as much." Pleased with herself, Amalí smiles, and her fingers pluck the fruit with intensified vigor.

A cloud of dust in the distance is the signal to stop working. It is six o'clock in the afternoon. A long cart arrives, pulled by a tractor. Laughing and screaming, the women climb onto it.

Three hundred boxes full of peppers are left neatly lined up in the fields. Acopio[4] will pick them up during the night. Nobody takes any peppers home. They are for export and constitute a valuable source of foreign exchange. Those that aren't exported will be sold cheaply at the vegetable stand at the Cooperative.

There is noise, chatter. The men from the rice fields also climb onto the long narrow wagon.

A loud voice can be heard over the confusion.

> The peasant "dance"
> In all its splendor
> Inspires the troubadour
> To a fine meditation.
> There is a *décima* on the road,
> In the thicket, and on the plain.

> There is a verse in the swamp
> Where life is difficult,
> And there is a rhyme hanging
> From every leaf of the palm tree.

It's Manuel, the quixote, who is singing. Everyone applauds him.

Behind us, in the bluish landscape where men and women have completed a hard day's work, we leave a silence broken only by the sound of birds and insects. A cloud of gray dust raised by the wagon as it moves along the road veils the landscape.

THE EVENING

Tall and broad-shouldered, this man is not made for the crowded kitchen where he moves about. Old but shiny pots hang from the walls, their lids wedged between slats.

He greets me casually. "Do you speak Russian?" He's René, Elena's husband.

The children come running in and lift the lids from the pots. The corn chowder is almost ready. It's a good thing, because everyone is hungry. Will Elena sit at the table? Certainly not!

Nene's children come over to watch the cartoons on television because they don't have a set at home. "I'll be the last one to get one, since I am the president of the Cooperative," Nene says.

The Cooperative, like all work centers, receives an allotted number of electric appliances which are sold on an easy-payment plan to the most deserving and needy peasants.

The eldest daughter, Zoraidita, twelve years old, washes the dishes. In her opinion, the local girls don't help much around the house, but certainly more than the boys who "only know how to bother people."

Elena and René agree that many peasants, themselves included, spoil their children. "It's because people of our generation, who were already adults when the Revolution triumphed, had miserable childhoods," René comments. "And taking pity on ourselves, we try to give our children a better life. So what happens? They take advantage of us. But they do help out some, bringing groceries in from the store, washing dishes, and helping out with the younger children. When it is time to harvest the tobacco, they work more and learn the technique. Eventually, they go to high school where they have lessons and also work in agricultural production half-days. There they learn to be responsible and understand that 'Manna doesn't fall from heaven.'"

The neighbor's child is playing with a large dog near the porch. Noticing that he's dirty, Elena picks him up and carries him off to give him a bath, bringing him back a while later, naked except for his shoes.

"I bathed him for you already, he was so dirty," she tells the child's mother as the latter approaches them and smothers the boy with kisses. "Here we help each other any way we can, and nobody gets offended," Elena comments.

The bright red sun seems to be disappearing slowly in the distance. A moonless night is falling.

A white owl flaps its wings and awakens a myriad insects with its strident cries. Scattered lights make it possible to count the bohíos. It is time for the domestic hustle and bustle, time to take the goat to the corral. Night life at the Cooperative begins.

Youngsters ride by on bicycles on their way to town, talking about judo. A message arrives that there will be a meeting with the delegate from the neighborhood's Popular Power Assembly[12] to discuss the status of neighborhood projects and petitions on Sunday.

The neighbor comes over to practice her sewing on Elena's machine; she's taking sewing lessons offered by the Federation. Adults walk by, books in hand, greeting everyone.

Powerful turbines, which push water through narrow canals to irrigate the fields of rice and tubers, begin to turn. A couple, arm in arm, disappears in the shadows on their way to the pond.

Zoraidita, wearing a sweet and peaceful expression, sleeps. She has never known poverty. And the meaning she will give to life is in her own hands. All the doors stand open!

The Soviet-made television set is a center of interest for Elena's children in the small, but immaculate bohío. Jørgen Schytte

"Good things take getting used to." Elena still does much of the laundry by hand, despite owning a new washing machine. Jørgen Schytte

The sweeping landscape where Cuban tobacco—the best in the world—is raised. MAYITO

Elena's neighbor uses the sewing machine while waiting for others to join the sewing class. INGER HOLT-SEELAND

Pastora and her husband Pablo flank Nene, president of the Cooperative during a break for a buchito. JØRGEN SCHYTTE

The tobacco barn. INGER HOLT-SEELAND

The leader of the Cooperative's chapter of the Federation of Cuban Women in her bohío. Most Cuban women feel no contradiction between religion, symbolized by the Christ on the wall, and Marxism, symbolized by the prominently displayed photograph of Che. INGER HOLT-SEELAND

Picking beans at the Celso Maragoto Cooperative is women's work. JØRGEN SCHYTTE

2

"What was the central idea, the point of the analyses and the efforts of this convention? The struggle for women's equality! The struggle for the complete integration of women into Cuban society! This is truly a historic battle. We believe this objective to be precisely what constitutes this convention's challenge, for in practice full equality of women still does not exist."

—FIDEL CASTRO
Closing address to the Second
Congress of the Federation
of Cuban Women

ISABEL/Homemaker

AGENDA

TOPIC: Interview with Isabel (Homemaker)

HOME ADDRESS: Reparto Miramar (Aristocratic residential section before the triumph of the revolution)

HUSBAND'S OCCUPATION: Civil servant

CHILDREN: A daughter, twenty years old, a third-year student in marine biology; and a son, eight years old, fourth grade.

REVOLUTIONARY PARTICIPATION: Organizer and activist in the social work of the Committees for the Defense of the Revolution (CDR). Member of the Financial Front and Solidarity Activist committees in coordination with the Federation of Cuban Women (FMC, Federación de Mujeres Cubanas).

AWARDS: Combatant Mother, Outstanding Cederista,* Outstanding Federada.†

Cederista, a member of a CDR.
†*Federada*, a member of the FMC.

In the small strip of garden in front of Isabel's house grows a variety of rich tropical flora: blushing carnations, sensuous night jasmine, and yerbabuena, a variety of the mint family indispensable to the typical Cuban drink *mojito*.[5]

The sidewalk and wide front porch have just been mopped. A burlap bag placed across the path reminds you to wipe your feet before you cross the wet surface. Four iron armchairs are tilted against the wall, and begonias hang vigorous, fresh, and healthy from clay pots.

Isabel opens the door without offering her hand. She is drying one hand on her apron and with the other removing a black tobacco cigarette from between her shapely lips.

She is wearing a blue tweed skirt and a white blouse with the sleeves rolled up to the elbows, into bands that accentuate her slender figure. Her olive complexion and dark eyes clash with her curly bleached hair. She is embarrassed to be caught out at such an awkward hour, the hour when housewives are beginning their daily chores.

The combination dining room-living room is spacious and rectangular. The furniture, in a style fashionable in America in the fifties, is somewhat delapidated. The walls display shelves of books, china, medium-sized art reproductions, among them "The Tropical Gypsy" by the Cuban painter Victor Manuel, and her husband's diploma, which is written out in fancy calligraphy. The portrait of Che with the bright star on his beret dominates the room.

The windowpanes are painted in bright primary colors in imitation of the gothic windows so abundant in colonial Cuban architecture.

The house is messy. "We stayed up late last night watching a movie," she explains as she begins to collect the overflowing ashtrays by the television set, "I really smoke a lot, you know." She wipes the top of a wide glass table with a skillful hand and clears away the morning's breakfast dishes. "Those children of mine are so messy!" She puts the chairs in their places. She serves some reheated coffee, and feeling a bit more secure, sits down to talk.

"I don't think my case is anything special. There are thousands of housewives involved in many diverse activities in the people's organizations. If there is a difference, it might be the fact that I joined the revolution rather late, in '70 or '71 . . ." She says all this quickly, without pausing for a breath, her mouth half open in a smile.

Her family and their social circle were well-to-do owners of apartments, houses, land, and businesses. They were lawyers, doctors, and engineers. "The word 'communism' horrified us. We were Catholics who went to confession and Mass on Sunday."

When the nationalization took place in 1960 the exodus of Cubans to the United States began. "I couldn't go. Pedro had joined the Revolution, and he would never have let me take Isabelita with me."

Between 1959 and 1960 the following laws were legislated: the first and second agrarian reform bills outlawing the *latifundio* and fixing maximum individual land ownership at 138 acres; a rent-control law that reduced rents by one half; an urban reform law that let many city dwellers become owners of the houses they were living in; and a bill providing for the nationalization through forced expropriation of all industrial and commercial enterprises in the country.

From that moment on, the United States government intensified its attacks on the revolution while increasing its support for Cuban exiles. More than any other factor, the above-mentioned laws were what caused some Cubans to leave.

"I still believe in God," Isabel continues, "but in my own way. In the end I was persuaded...by the Revolution...because of what it did. I'm like Saint Thomas: 'Seeing is believing.' It was a long process, but maybe that's why I'm so resolute."

"When you speak of 'what the revolution did,' what are you referring to?"

"We can never go back to the past. Injustice was rampant in the government of thieves and murderers this country suffered most of its life. Not one, not a single one of the earlier governments is exempt from this judgment! And the social class to which I belonged was what gave them their support.

"When the Revolution arrived, it swept all this away, committing, it's true, dozens of errors, but always with a deep sense of justice and honor."

"What part did Pedro play in your spectacular change of mind?"

"None, I think. What's more, his lectures bothered me," she says, as memories she appears to have buried bring a sad smile to her face, "to such an extent that the growing conflict put us on the edge of

divorce. There was a time we lived like strangers in this big house—
physical estrangement—rage. I even started to believe I was in love
with someone else...Now I know I was only looking for an escape.
Thank goodness, Pedro is a good man, patient and very compassion-
ate. Otherwise I might have lost him altogether."

"How did this situation affect your little girl? Didn't you run into
problems?"

"Inevitably. When Pedro was at work, I had visitors who came to
throw wood on the fire, to speculate about what was going on: what
if the revolution failed, what if the Americans attacked. They painted
my daughter's future black. It was almost a conspiracy. Isabelita was
a witness to this and other situations in which my conduct conflicted
with what she was learning at school, and with her father's example
and the influence of her environment."

"What was that environment like?"

"The environment? Just imagine! The people...delighted with
the new, under constant tension because of the daily attacks, and
with a program of unending work ahead, because in this country
everything was yet to be done! Fidel's fiery speeches electrified the
masses. The word 'revolution' was ever-present, revolutionary an-
thems, revolutionary radio and television programs, posters,
books...everything revolutionary! What makes you think the girl
could ever have believed I was right?"

"So what finally happened?"

"I recall now that ever since Isabelita's birth I had had plans to
marry her off to a man of a certain social standing. All the marriages
in my family met this condition, with the exception of my own, because Pedro was not rich. In short, though I had gone against the
wishes of my family, I had, deep down, the idea that happiness can
only be built on a solid economic foundation. It was one of my
myths. But who could I find to marry Isabelita if there were no rich
men left in Cuba?" She takes a vigorous puff on her cigarette; her eyes
seem to speak of the enormous changes she has gone through. "Then
she became a Pioneer, and so every day I was losing her respect. I
could no longer ignore the fact that I was struggling in vain against
reality. I couldn't sleep knowing there would be more confronta-

tions the next day. It was a losing battle. My nerves were completely shot."

"Were you alone through all that anguish? Didn't you have anybody to turn to?"

"Life has its ironies. The help and comfort I should've got from a priest came from Manolo, an old communist, a party member since the thirties and president of our local Committee. Manolo started coming by to talk. He was very earnest and sincere. He'd ask me what I didn't understand, what seemed good to me and what seemed bad. Finally, Manolo plucked me out of the darkness. His arguments held water; mine didn't. He defended the rights of the people; I was defending the rights of a certain class. . . . He even got me to recognize that."

"After Manolo converted you, what did you do next?"

"Well, I don't know that you can call it 'conversion.' It was just a question of no longer being able to ignore reality. One day I was invited to a Committee meeting. I thought it might be interesting, so I went, and the people made me feel very welcome. I went back whenever I could until the day the woman in charge of the Educational Front got sick and Manolo asked if I wouldn't help out, just for a few days. . .and I said I would. I love interacting with people so much, solving the problems that crop up. . .I got into the action, put an end to my isolation and signed up for the Committee."

"What motivated your initial rejection of the CDR?"

"I had the idea that their primary objective was political repression. That seemed logical, in a way: Hadn't they been created to combat counterrevolution? But things changed, and Committee programs expanded until they became what they are now, social service programs in health, education, social work. . ."

"So today we can say you're one hundred percent revolutionary?"

"Well, no!" Waving her hands for emphasis, she says, "I don't think there are many people who can call themselves that—Fidel, Che, Raul. . .I don't know, they're very few. But there certainly are millions of us on the path to becoming revolutionaries. One has to be realistic and understand that we all have weaknesses as a result of our past education. Personally, I can tell you..."

"Give me an example of such a weakness."

"The...racial problem. Do you think I'd like to see Isabelita going out with a black man? Not in a thousand years! So I ask myself, am I racist? I certainly was before. My milieu was racist. Everyone was. And today, in spite of that, I have colleagues and friends who are black. When I talk to them, I don't think about the fact that they are black. But when it hits close to home, I react violently. Maybe it's instinct or prejudice. I feel repulsed. It's a feeling I can't master, although I know it's...improper, not the way one human being deserves to be treated by another. I could give you many other examples of my defects and of everyone else's, too."

"Machismo is in contradiction to revolutionary ideology. How many people in this country aren't sexist?"

"You can count them on your fingers," she says, and counts them. "We are all sexist to a greater or lesser degree. Very few people deserve to count themselves among the 'guilt-free.' Does this mean that all those who are sexist are not revolutionaries? No, it doesn't. They're revolutionaries to the point of wanting to give their lives for freedom, not only here in Cuba, but in other countries, countries we feel are our brothers."

"What do you mean by that, Isabel? What if your son or your daughter decided to go and fight for the freedom of blacks in, let's say, Africa?"

"You think I haven't asked myself that question? God forbid! But if it should happen, I swear to you that I would be among the first to encourage them to do their duty."

"Encourage them? Duty? Why defend the freedom of a race you don't find fit to marry your children?"

You didn't understand, did you? You don't understand that we are a people in revolution, in other words, a people full of contradictions. There are a lot of people who think as you do that as soon as you call yourself a revolutionary you are washed clean and make the grade as a 'new man' or 'new woman.' But we are plagued by defects, errors, doubts. No one changes overnight, it comes slowly. There are many, many things that are difficult to assimilate—like the idea of my daughter with a black man. Even though I'd accept my children giving their lives for them, for their freedom—and I mean it—I just can't help carrying these old attitudes around with me. They are the focus of a long struggle to purify—excuse me!—revolutionize ourselves, each according to his own capability, understanding, and sensibility. Has it ever occurred to you that we even have to change our vocabulary? It takes a lot of effort not to start talking about 'purity' again."

"In addition to being discriminatory, isn't this attitude of yours toward blacks romantic and paternalistic?"

"You're trying to confuse me," Isabel says, standing up. "How can we avoid viewing them still with a certain sense of superiority, we who belong to the older generation? Aren't you aware of what a Negro used to be worth? Don't you know that they were not allowed to sit on park benches in many of the country's parks, that they couldn't go to first-class restaurants or clubs. Remember the little 'For Whites Only'?" She sits down to light a cigarette. "Today, however, you go to a school and you'll see little black and white kids completely at ease with one another. They date without its being news to anyone. Even I might be able to get used to it."

A street vendor's cry is heard from the street, "Green onions! Fresh green onions and okra!" Isabel gets up quickly and calls to the man as he goes by on his bicycle. She buys not only his green onions, but some parsley and garlic, too.

We take the groceries into the big, comfortable kitchen where a few tiles have fallen off the walls. The coffee filter, heavy with humid coffee grounds, waits for the second round of hot water to be poured through it. "You have to get all you can out of it," Isabel explains. "We can't get another ration until Saturday." We drink the classic *buchito*, a tiny black cup of coffee, and she lights another cigarette, which she places at the corner of her mouth, shutting one eye because of the bothersome smoke.

"Hear that? That's all we needed. She's mistreating her little boy again." She sighs, without removing the cigarette from her mouth. The voice of a neighbor woman at her wit's end comes in through the light-filled window. The boy's protests turn to sobs when he realizes his mother is not going to let him out to play.

With barely concealed disgust Isabel says she disapproves of the way her neighbor treats the boy. "This scene is repeated over and over again. Consuelo is a frustrated woman who takes it out on the kid. She dreams of going back to work like she did before she got married. The husband approves, but the father-in-law won't hear of it. He calls working married women whores and gives Consuelo a monthly stipend, which is probably more than she could earn on the job. She's caught in the trap of the home that is smothering her," Isabel concludes, scrubbing furiously at the milkpot.

"You were once an airline stewardess and later worked at the airport. What finally made you stop working?"

"It's difficult to confess painful things that you are always trying to forget. My defense mechanisms work to perfection," she says, trying to find the thread of her story.

"When I married Pedro, I quit flying and went to work in the office at the airport until the Betancourt incident in 1966.[6] I don't know if you remember the period when the United States loosed a fierce campaign against the revolutionary government; it offered asylum to the war criminals of Batista's government; it established the economic blockade; CIA agents blew up the steamship *La Coubre*,[7] killing many people; the Bay of Pigs; the bombers—I'll never forget the date, it was the fifteenth of April 1961, they dropped a bomb right here that shattered all the windowpanes in the neighborhood.[8] Then came the October Crisis in 1962[9] which brought the world to the brink of a third world war. I remember the American warships along the coast, so close that we could see them from the terrace on the roof. That was really something! What were we talking about? Oh, about the airport.

"The airport is a strategic point, and it was already in style to hijack planes. They called it 'air piracy,' and it was spreading all over the world. There were attempts to dynamite planes in flight but they were unsuccessful, except for the one Barbados flight in 1976, which actually did go up.[10] That was why the government decided to fire all personnel known to be unsympathetic to the revolution...and I was one of them. Of course, I could've found another job without much trouble because I spoke English, and at that time it wasn't like now, when anyone and everyone speaks a foreign language. But I didn't want to go back to work, I didn't want to cooperate with the Revolution, and this is what weighs so heavily on me now.

WHO IS TO BLAME?

"As soon as I felt ready to go back to work, Aunt Nena got sick on me, but that's another story. Do you want to hear it? O.K., she was like an aunt to me, although she really wasn't an aunt. She grew up with my grandmother and was always very good to us. I had to take her in. She didn't live many years after that, may she rest in peace, but how she suffered! Poor woman! It was because her family abandoned her. They left her alone in a mansion she couldn't take care of—Louis XV-style chairs collecting dust. They took all the jewels and money, and sent her a few pesos every once in a while, which didn't get her far at all. After a while, even that stopped. They forgot she existed. They didn't even send a telegram on her birthday.

"So she started selling the valuables to swindlers, furniture, carpets, and by the time she got sick, that house, once so luxurious, was pitifully empty and sad."

"And her pension...?"

"She had a right to an old-age pension and to a rent for the property confiscated from her family, but she refused to accept them...out of pride. She firmly believed that the Revolution, not her family, was to blame for her abandonment. It's also possible that she didn't accept them because she thought, like so many others, that the Revolution would not last.

"And so, taking care of her kept me from going back to work. Pedrito was born. I started working for the Committees and the Federation, and perhaps out of a certain laziness on my part I slowly lost the necessary, uh, 'training' as they say, to go back again and face the street, the buses, the heat..."

The morning is flying by. Isabel has to go and buy a few groceries in order to fix lunch before her children come home from school at noon.

THE GROCERY STORE

"Hurry up Isabel, they've got potatoes," yells a woman as she rushes past us.

"Today's a bad day to go to the store," Isabel says as she quickens her pace. "The first and the fifteenth are the days allotments are distributed and everyone swarms into the store."

Two women in lively conversation on their way back from the store greet us as they pass. The short black woman, still young, barely fits into her tight red pants. Sweating copiously, she is pushing an old baby carriage brimming with groceries, with an earthenware crock containing lard perilously balanced on top. The other, a mulatto a bit older than the first, struggles with two enormous baskets in which the heel of an unwrapped loaf of bread is visible.

The store does not provide containers, so shoppers must bring bottles or crocks for the butter and oil. These products are sold from big plastic tubs. Paper for wrapping some items has recently become available, but shoppers still bring baskets for bulky items, such as fruits and vegetables. "Cuba buys paper with foreign currency," Isabel comments, "so it has to be saved."

"This is intolerable!" is the first thing we hear as we come closer to the line of people, boxes, and home-made shopping carts in front of the store. "Intolerable!" the same male voice continues. "It's not for nothing that things aren't going well in this country. They don't even know how to organize a piddling little grocery store."

"From what I see, Antonio, you've forgotten how hungry you used to be," a woman breaks in aggressively. "Don't I always say, yesterday's hungriest are today's most demanding, and they don't contribute a thing. They don't even come out on Sundays to sweep the block,[11] and they don't have guts enough to stand up at neighborhood Assembly Association meetings,[12] which is where they ought to take their problems."

"Don't pay any attention to him, honey," another woman interrupts, speaking in the same tone of voice. "He's just saying that to get in the good graces of the people who are paying him to do their shopping."

"That's partly true," says a friendly old man getting up from the box on which he has been sitting. "But there's truth to what Antonio says, too. If he doesn't like to speak up at the assemblies, why doesn't someone else do it? They've got to get more help in here, because with the bread line, the *jaba* plan,[13] the produce, and everything else, the line just isn't moving. Cheo and Maria are going to get sick over it."

"Ain't nobody gonna hurry me or give me no nervous breakdown," Cheo the shopkeeper says without taking the dead cigarette out of his mouth. "And whoever don't like it can git theirself to another store.

Cuz I ain't hiring nobody else. Maria's all the help I need. And anybody tells me different's just plain stupid, cuz we's the perfect marriage," he says, smiling so that all his teeth show. "She's got the head
for numbers and I have the muscle"—he shows his biceps—"to carry
the loads. So let's just calm down there."

"Listen, Cheo," Isabel interrupts, "get to work and stop making
speeches. I'll help with the bread." Without losing a minute Isabel
goes behind the counter and begins taking loaves of bread out of a
white bag.

"Hey, Maria," Isabel says, "does the bread get marked down for
the quota books?"

"What for?" Maria answers. "There's always enough."

The bread line moves right along, thanks to Isabel. Cheo and
Maria catch her infectious enthusiasm.

"PLIP, PLOP"

Two ladies, of the sort who have "come down" in the world, are
standing somewhat apart from the line and talking.

"Oh, Olga! Yesterday my biorhythm was at its peak, and you
won't believe the things that happened to me! In the morning I took
my puppy out to go pee-pee and when I was in front of the Scholars'
Building an old man comes out and says, 'Heeeey lady! I'm putting
out dog poison because I'm the one who cleans up around here, and
if you think I'm going to pick up those little mounds of —' "

"You're kidding, Maria! He didn't really say THAT! What a
foulmouth!" Olga exclaims. "I certainly hope you told him off."

"Not a word, dear. There's no defense against vulgarity. I left as
quickly as I could. Lilly, the wife of the painter who lives around the
corner, called me later and invited me out to the Coppelia.[14] We got
there at ten and they still weren't open, so I went up to a little mulatto
I saw standing there and said, 'Excuse me, young lady, what time do
they open?' But the little brat didn't even answer me...They finally
opened at fifteen after. So we went in and sat down.

"So the girl came over and I told her, 'I'll have a chocolate sundae
with...' and she walked right off without letting me finish. There
were three kinds of chocolate ice cream. When she came back with
the sundae, I said, 'Comrade,' real nice, just like that, 'Comrade, you
didn't let me finish speaking. I was going to ask you for malted

chocolate, not plain chocolate...' 'Well, we're out,' she said with a
blank face. 'But if it's on the menu?' I insisted. 'Ask for a different
one, then, if you like,' she said. So I asked her for a marble fudge
sundae, and from where I was sitting I saw her take the syrup and go
like this 'plip' on top of the ice cream, then she took the marshmallow
cream and gave it a little shot 'plop,' that you could barely even see. I
felt like telling her, 'What's this, some kind of decoration like the
strawberry they used to put on top?' And Lilly, who couldn't stand it
any longer, said, 'Oh, stop it, Maria, I'll buy you another ice cream.' "

THE OLD MEN'S CLUB

A group of old men are enjoying the shade of a linden tree in front of
the store. One of the boxes in the circle where they are sitting is not
taken: "How strange that Joaquin isn't here yet!" I ask them if they
aren't losing their turn in line by sitting there. "No, ma'am, our places
are saved." They all stand up and the one who is speaking puts his arm
around my shoulders, another affectionate Cuban custom. "At our
age we're not in such a hurry, you see, everything comes in time.
Even death and fresh air are things that should be enjoyed. We're in
the habit of meeting here for a little while every morning when the
bread comes. And in the afternoon we come by again to see what's on
the list of unrationed products...Then we sit and talk some more."

When we leave, the store is still full of people. The basket of
potatoes is the hardest to carry. On the way we talk about the rationed and unrationed products, each one being announced daily on
the store's blackboard.

Today the list of unrationed products included, among other things,
noodles, Russian applesauce, sauerkraut, corn syrup, potatoes, radishes,
lettuce, powdered milk, wheat and corn flour, various soup mixes,
yoghurt, butter, and eggs.

The rationed products, though they are rationed on a monthly
basis, are announced as the store receives them. They are rice, fresh
and canned milk, meat, shortening, beans, coffee, sugar, soap, de-
tergent, Iraqi dates and out-of-season vegetables. Today there were
dietary supplements of oranges and malangas (a tuber resembling a
sweet potato) on a separate list for children, the elderly, and the sick.

Isabel is of the opinion that the rationing reflects shortages rather
than dire need, even though it has fostered appreciable irritation

among housewives who find it difficult to vary their menus with limited ingredients. On the other hand, "Many of the people you see complaining that the monthly allotments of rice and other products aren't enough are the ones who throw their leftovers away because they refuse to eat 'warmed-over' food. The same is true of bread. If it wasn't baked that morning, they won't touch it."

The lunch she's fixing today consists of cole slaw, white rice, leftover navy beans, french fries, and a hash for which she chops an onion and red and green chile peppers. "If onions weren't rationed, I'd throw in two," Isabel says. She crushes the garlic in an old wooden mortar and then sautés everything in a frying pan with shortening, bay leaf, cumin, and oregano. She beats four eggs in a mixing bowl and adds four tablespoons of *gofio* (flour from corn that has been roasted before being ground). This form a dough that she fries separately in scant shortening until well done. She removes this from the pan and fries a little bit of ground meat which she had previously seasoned with lemon, salt, and pepper. She adds the meat and *gofio* to the onions and chili peppers, adds half a cup of dry red wine, half a can of tomatoe puree, covers it tight, and leaves it to simmer over a low fire.

"The trick of stretching meat with *gofio* is quite common. Anyway, you can't really tell the difference between them. *Gofio* is very nourishing. The Canary Islanders eat it all the time, and they're as strong as bulls."

A neighbor comes to the door and asks to borrow some butter. "I was on night patrol for the Committee,"[15] she says to explain why she didn't get up in time to make it to the grocery store before the line became too long. Isabel takes the opportunity to give her three pounds of rice for which the neighbor will give Isabel three packages of cigarettes when her turn comes to collect the allotment. As the neighbor leaves, she says she's going to fix cod for lunch.

Isabel turns up her nose and tells me that her family, like most families, doesn't like fish from cold ocean currents such as cod and mackerel, because of the high oil content. They eat it only to increase their protein intake.

"If you compared yourself to a working woman, what would be the pros and cons?"

"Everything is the color of the lens you look through," she says taking a cautious puff on her cigarette. "If as a housewife my life is

calmer because I have only the house to look after, the working woman
has the advantage of the pass which gives her access to the *jaba* plan
and priority in buying electric appliances. She has a salary, will get a
pension, and has a prestigious social position. The truth is I can't
complain. Ever since I joined the Federation and the Committee, I feel
fulfilled. In any case, both the working woman and I have problems
with services like gas delivery—it takes several days between the time
you order a tank of gas for the stove and the time it's delivered.
Whenever anything breaks down, the stove, the iron, the television
or whatever, it's ages before you can get anyone out to fix it. More-
over, replacement parts and other household items such as bathroom
hardware or fabric for reupholstering furniture are getting harder and
harder to find. There also aren't enough dry cleaners, but Fidel talked
about resolving that particular problem at the Federation's Third
Congress."

*"Returning to electric appliances, doesn't Pedro have the right to buy
them as a worker?"*

"Yes, men and women have the same right to purchase television
sets, refrigerators, fans, and other appliances. But a man can't buy a
washer or a sewing machine so long as there is one woman at his
workplace who needs one. Women get preferential treatment in that
case."

"Discriminating against men?"

"Well, yes, but you mustn't forget that the working women in
Cuba still carry the largest workload because men don't assume the
responsibility around the house that, for instance, the younger generation of men will have to take. It's good to remember what Fidel
said about that."

Isabel gets out a scrapbook of newspaper clippings and reads:
" 'If in human society you have to have any inequality, if in human
society you have to have any privilege, then they ought to be in
women's favor.' Fidel Castro, closing speech to the Second Congress
of the Federation of Cuban Women, November 29, 1974."

"Who takes care of the household accounts?"

Isabel says she recognizes that money is an important issue, but
that Pedro, "like most Cuban men," gives her an envelope with his

salary in it and expects her to manage it. He spends very little—gas for the car, fifty cents a day for lunch at the employees' cafeteria where he works, and an occasional beer with friends. "He even quit smoking," Isabel says, "not so much because he was afraid of getting cancer, but because of the hole cigarettes leave in your pocket and the fact that I smoke too much."

In Cuba cigarettes and loose tobacco are rationed and sold at twenty centavos a package. Every consumer has the right to four packs of cigarettes and four packages of tobacco a month. The consumer can buy additional cigarettes at $1.60 a pack, and cigars at $0.60 to $0.80 a package, depending on the quality. These prices make tobacco a luxury item.

"It seems that Pedro is a model husband."

"He's very good. . . but model? He's too messy. When he smoked, he used to throw the butts on the floor. Now it's the newspaper, his shirts, his shoes. You can find them anywhere but where they belong. When I scold him, he says that I'm home all day and that when he comes home from work he's tired. He says it as though I just lazed around all day. It bothers me because when I worked he helped me although there was no Family Code. When I tell him I could go back to work any day, he goes into a fit of laughter because he doesn't believe I'm capable of doing it."

"Doesn't he give you all the money in exchange for your dependence on him?"

"If Pedro wasn't who he is, I'd say yes, but from what I've told you about him today I'm sure you realize that he doesn't think that way. When I worked, he also gave me his salary."

A slam of the door and the sound of light feet gliding across the tiles in the living room announce Pedrito.

"Hurry up, Mom, we're hungry. I brought Raulito home for lunch. We're gonna play ball."

"This is my son," Isabel says with evident pride as she takes the little boy into her arms. The boy doesn't pay any attention to the introduction and continues insisting on being served so that he can go out and play. Isabel snaps to: she runs from the dining room to the kitchen and vice versa; she brings him water—and the little tyrant asks for more. He demands the heel because he doesn't like the soft center of the loaf of bread and asks, "Why didn't you fry me any bananas?" Isabel flies to prepare them.

ISA/University Student

"*Buenas tardes,*" comes the fresh sound of Isabelita's voice. She's medium height, olive complexion, and slim like her mother. Her long hair is a natural chestnut brown. Her fingernails and toenails are fire-engine red, her eyes made-up. A seashell called a *polimita*[16] hangs on a fine strip of leather around her long neck. She dresses simply—pants, a T-shirt, comfortable sandals. Isabel introduces her in a hurry and runs back to the kitchen.

"Call me Isa," she says, and kisses her brother. "You wild thing, you," she says, pulling playfully at his hair.

We sit down at the table just as the "wild thing" and his little friend finish eating. Isabel comes back, "Here's my treasure," she says, hands full of the bananas she has just fried for her son. But "it's too late." The boys shoot out the door with their mouths full, slamming it with all their might.

"There goes the 'new man,' " Isa says with ironic solemnity. "At least he'll eat lunch at school once he finishes primary grades." Then she adds, in front of her mother, who shows no signs of protest, that most parents are incapable of raising their children properly, that the children who are in day care first, who then go straight into a school where lunch is served, and who have scholarships, are better prepared for life because they are more responsible.

Isabelita calls her room a "big cave." The walls are all painted white and papered over with suggestive posters and strings of necklaces in bunches made from tropical seeds and other "weird things." A mirror covers the whole closet door, which is half closed on the abundant mess behind it. A guitar, a radio phonograph, a nearly burnt-out candle on a green bottle, and her many books are splayed on the home-made rug by the mattress where we sit. Three random titles: Frantz Fanon's *Black Faces, White Masks*, José Lezama Lima's *Anthology of Cuban Poetry*; Raul Valdes Vivo's *Ethiopia: The Unknown Revolution*. Her personal effects, such as make-up, are stacked on a low shelf. The convenience and informality of Isa's set-up bring us closer together.

"I'm discovering your family's secrets," I assure her.

"Learning is the essence of human nature, but we rarely succeed in satisfying our need for it. We are steeped in ignorance before the terrible spaces of the universe that surrounds us; we know very little about the body and even less about the mind. As far as my family's secrets go...Dostoyevsky once said something like 'fiction will never outdo reality.' "

"How are your studies going? What's happening at the university?"

"I'm in my third year, specializing in marine biology, and I'm a member of the Union of Young Communists. These activities exact a systematic and conscientious effort on my part, because it's unheard-of for a Young Communist to have poor grades.

"The university is inflexible as far as studies go and will expel anyone who does not take all the requirements, even if it's only sports. You have to participate in sports, and what's more, you have to be good at them. The principle of integrated education is what's behind all this. Education should be integrated with reality, not in quotation marks.

"We consider the student to be a social being with rights and responsibilities that include educating and preparing himself to the best of his capabilities to serve the Revolution. It is the Revolution that pays for his studies and provides the means by which he can develop himself. It is the Revolution that deepens his understanding and knowledge of current political problems through the people's organizations, and permits him to discover and develop the potentials that are his as a social being."

"What do you have to do to be a Young Communist?"

"First, you have to get good grades, be an example to society, volunteer for guard duty, attend the Study Center once a month, attend the meetings of the Grassroots Committee—in which we deal with particular student cases, political problems, problems in the home and with the professors, and so on. These meetings occur approximately twice a month.

"YCU militants are a natural talent pool from which the Party draws. For this reason we are required to demonstrate moral, political, and ideological qualities such as allegiance to our country,

to the working class, to socialism, and to the international pro-
letariat."

"Isn't there also volunteer work?"

"I forgot, at least once a month we clean classrooms, playing
fields, whatever needs to be done."

*"Do you think you could tell me about your mother without being too
indulgent?"*

"Why not? We have to free ourselves of false piety, and all artificial emotion. It's the only way life can be natural again . . .

"My mother is a very intelligent woman who was able to make
the leap from hardened reactionary to enthusiastic revolutionary, all
without dropping the sexist conceptions that are the heritage left her
by our family, in addition, of course, to this house in which we are
now talking. The only reason they didn't take the house with them is
because they couldn't.

"Nevertheless, Mama thinks she is free. She doesn't understand
that with every passing day the household enslaves her more. She
tries to keep the house straight, but that lasts only until my little
brother and father come home. She has an unhealthy meticulousness
about the floors, the furniture, dusting. I'm not sure why I associate
her with those people who spend the day washing their hands. If she
got a job and made all of us responsible for the housework, it wouldn't
be such a big deal for anyone and we'd certainly keep things better
organized. I don't let her do anything in here. This is my world.

"It's equally important to recognize that she works very hard.
Not only is she greatly respected on the fronts for which she works,
but people come to her from other organizations almost every day to
ask her help in solving problems. This is what she lives for, in her
own way, of course."

We hear Isabel come up the stairs. She hands Isa a letter, "It's
from Aunt Sophie," she says, her face glowing. She picks up a sweater
left lying on top of some books, and leaves.

" 'I haven't written since I got back,' " Isa reads, adding that
Aunt Sophie lives in New York. " 'As I got on the plane I couldn't
hold back my tears. I miss all of you in Cuba so much, the sun, the
beaches, the music, the jokes, the rhythm in the way people move.
What a contrast! Here we live closed off, spiritually as well as physi-

cally, without the communication we Latins are used to. On top of the solitude and the cold, we are afraid, afraid to lose a little of all the things we possess, afraid of not being able to get what we don't already have, because that is what, as a rule, everyone here aspires to...'

"This letter is incredible!" Isa says with surprise. She explains that she had given up reading her aunt's letters because they were "so banal, all about clothes, cars, and other stupid things, with ridiculous color photos for documentary proof.

"Four months ago she spent a week with us. She arrived forgiving us for the way we lived, criticizing everything that was merely plain or sufficient, the houses in need of paint, the public transportation, the old cars...So I confronted her! 'Auntie, do you remember that fine whorehouse around the corner from the store? You told me never to go near it and made up stories about witches and magic. Auntie, do you remember Consuelo and the other lady who used to clean house for you? And Lazarito, the little black boy who used to run errands for you? Well, in that fine house there aren't any more witches; a normal family lives there. Consuelo has her pension and the children help her out. I haven't seen the other lady. And Lazarito, who works for the Party—I'm not sure where—just finished studying for a career. Now children run around in school uniforms, confident in the future, confident that they won't die of hunger or lack of medical attention!' Aunt Sophie didn't know what to say. Afterward, I was sorry I had talked like that to her, I'm not used to that sort of thing."

"What are the major religious, political and sexual differences between your mother's generation and your own?"

"My generation has no such thing as a religious conflict because from the time we were very little we received a Marxist education. My mother's generation has had to move from dogmatic concepts to an understanding of dialectical materialism, but many of them got stuck halfway. My mother, for example, continues to believe in God and that there are certain studies, attitudes, and behaviors appropriate for women, all according to inherited patterns. She's a bit racist, very sexist, and with regard to questions of sex she's fairly old-fashioned. But if you subject her to a more rigorous analysis, it becomes clear that she was practically part of the vanguard in her youth. What a paradox! She became an airline stewardess against the wishes of my grandparents because 'girls of good family' didn't work. Breaking with tradition, she married my father, who was neither rich nor Catholic and, to top it off, divorced. Her not having a church wedding caused an enormous split in the family. Yet she faced all this by herself. She stood her ground. It just slays me to think of Mom and Dad dating with chaperones. I'm convinced they didn't make love until after they were married."

"What was your sexual education like?"

"You know my mother and her taboos, so it won't surprise you that I didn't learn anything at home. And at school, only what I could get out of anatomy and biology classes.

"In this respect, a great mistake has been made with youth, by not offering us information and guidance when we needed it.

"The result: an excess of sexual freedom. Why blame us for the faults of our education? We've had no choice but to learn about it first hand, speculating, anxiously searching for an answer so essential to our development.

"Sexual education is the one area in which the religious indoctrinations of the past has maintained an influence within a process that should have done away with such an anachronism long ago, because revolution is change and Marxism is science."

"How important to you is virginity?"

"If you put that question to a man, his answer gives him away immediately.

"The great predominance of sexism before the Revolution with its widespread double standard, now in retreat, prescribed virginity for women while men were granted all the liberties.

"Today guys aren't very worried about virginity and are open-minded about it when they get married. Otherwise, they'd have to go out looking for a virgin like Diogenes with his lantern. They are the ones who have made sure there aren't any virgins, and I don't think it's the source of many problems. What *is* important is that the new man, the one we communists hope to create, put the emphasis on the seriousness of sexual relations, that he think more about that and less about the hymen."

"How is the responsibility for contraceptives shared?"

"It isn't. The inconvenience always falls on the woman. In general, men think it's a woman's responsibility."

"What do you and your parents do in your spare time?"

"My spare time is insignificant. What little I have I spend reading, or I may go to the theatre for amusement. Three times a week I get up earlier than usual and jog to the beach, which is about a kilometer away, swim a little, and then come jogging back. I wouldn't call that spare time, though.

"My parents and my little brother are addicted to television. Daddy almost always falls asleep watching westerns or Soviet war films. Every once in a while they'll take a Sunday and go to Lenin Park. Two or three times a year they'll go to a show and eat out. . . an occasional wedding, a birthday, that's how they spend their lives.

"Since you haven't asked me if I have a boyfriend, let me tell you that I do not," Isa concludes.

We go down to the dining room. Isabel looks very happy sitting at the table covered with papers, talking to two women from the Federation. They are sorting papers and taking notes.

Isa is anxious to get going. She has the afternoon free, and somebody waiting for her. She says goodbye with a quick kiss.

Steadily, bit by bit, under the sun that lights the way, her footfall fades until it is lost in the echoes of the long street. . .

Cheo and Maria in the bodega. Blackboards list rationed and unrationed products available for purchase. JØRGEN SCHYTTE

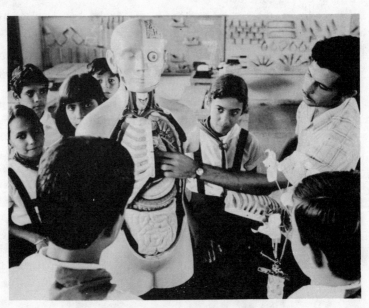

A biology class in a Cuban elementary school. Children must now complete nine years of school. JØRGEN SCHYTTE

Machismo *is dying, but not dead. How many people does Isbabel think are not sexist? "You can count them on your fingers," she says.* JØRGEN SCHYTTE

Housewives at an adult education class sponsored by the Federation of Cuban Women. JØRGEN SCHYTTE

A party, high up in the mountains of the Escambray, organized by the Federation of Cuban Women in honor of the author during research for this book. INGER HOLT-SEELAND

Cuban young people relaxing. JØRGEN SCHYTTE

Cuban workers earn the right to purchase scarce appliances by outstanding performance on the job. This couple is proud of the signs of their achievements. JØRGEN SCHYTTE

The old in the shadow of the new. New apartments not only provide better living accommodations, but preserve land for agricultural uses. JØRGEN SCHYTTE

Companionship among Isabelita's friends in the Young Communists is close and warm. MAYITO

3

"Exploitation is what women and workers have had in common since ancient times."

—*FERNANDO AUGUSTO BEBEL*

PAULINA/Factory Worker

If you visit old Havana with open eyes, overlooking the filth and neglect, you will discover mysteries and the enchantment of the unexpected: Cobblestone streets, artistic balconies with French doors, brilliant stained-glass windows, and century-old wrought-iron work by long forgotten artisans.

The plaza in front of the Cathedral, an important Cuban baroque construction, is an intimate and dignified square charged with history that takes its name from the Cathedral. This square saw the arrival in 1796 and the departure for Spain in 1898 of the supposed ashes of Christopher Columbus. In 1820 it saw the arrival of Bianchini silver, oils by Vernay, and copies of Rubens and Murillo, all for the Cathedral's adornment. It has been the setting for the ancestral rites of African slaves, performed to the beat of drums and mysterious song:

Goodbye, Goodbye,
Goodbye, my mother Hganga.
I'm going up the hill.
I'll cross the seven seas.
I'm going up there.
Nsulo,
Courtesy Ntoto on high.

It has been the site of virtual orgies of pirates and invading privateers. More recently the Ninth Symphony was directed by Leopold Stokowsky there, and on Saturdays it is the site of a crafts fair with all its music and color.

Serene and inspiring, the Plaza de Armas lies in front of the Palacio de los Capitanes Generales and the Castillo de la Fuerza, whose highest tower holds the Girardilla, the symbol of Havana, the statue of a woman, the first recognized work of sculpture by a Cuban artist.

Guarding the port are the Castillo de la Punta and the Castillo del Luminoso Murro, flanking the Fortaleza de la Cabana which every night at nine fires a cannon, a century-old tradition dating from the days when the city closed its gates in the ramparts that girdled it.

The ramparts were torn down when the days of piracy were over, and construction of the Malecon was begun, a cement wall that hugs the ocean from the foot of the bay to the newer part of Havana. Here on summer nights, until the dawn, people talk, fish and fall in love.

The growth of Havana to a city of two million inhabitants began with a surge of peasants from the countryside and of residents from small and medium-sized cities.

The flood of immigrants caused the city to spread eastward. Bursting its colonial bounds, it pierced the Bay Tunnel, flowed down the Via Monumental, steeped twelve months a year in flowering oleander, and invaded twenty kilometers of coastline, from the Castillo del Morro down a ten-kilometer stretch of white beach edging warm, clear, and shallow waters.

Midway along this route is the stone sentinel of Cojimar, a fishing village that heroically resisted the onslaught of English troops when they captured Havana in the eighteenth century. In our time it has been the backdrop for the life of Anselmo Hernandez, the gaunt fisherman whom Ernest Hemingway immortalized in his novel *The Old Man and the Sea*.

Within sight of Cojimar, a mammoth housing development, Alamar, is under construction. Here, the clothing factory, which is just one of many such installations, attracts our attention because of the large number of women workers.

THE WORKING WOMAN

This modern one-story building has huge windowpanes that flood the factory with light and allow the nearby ocean to send its salty breeze to the six hundred women who earn their living within the factory walls.

Paulina, the director, is black, very black, small and neat, and a fresh flower is pinned to her modest blouse. The strength of her character shows in her prudence and confidence. She wears her fifty-four years with dignity.

In her office the sound of the sewing machines is muted; the cries of the children in the daycare center are much clearer. The papers on her desk are stacked in careful symmetry. There are empty ashtrays on the long conference table, and awards the factory won in its struggle to increase production are hanging on the walls.

"This is a new factory. It was built in 1977 and I was given the honor of managing it. I think I'll retire here, although I hope that never happens.

"I am the grandaughter of slaves and the child of workers. My father was a tailor, and my mother worked in a tobacco factory, which is where I earned my first centavos...I was underage. There was work for only four or five months a year. The rest of the time we spent at home helping Papa, which is where I learned to sew. It's what I've done all my life.

"For women it was always difficult to hold on to a job in a miserable economy where work was given out to whoever charged the least. I've also found myself in the position of having to quit a job because of the amorous advances of one of the bosses. This kind of blackmail was par for the course. Either you put out for him or you lost the job.

"Because of the abusive treatment by management we were forced to strike quite frequently. Not a day went by that one of the shops wasn't out on strike, with meetings and demonstrations in the street, which the police repressed with beatings that sometimes didn't stop short of murder.

"So, I've seen a lot of changes. We used to live in a solar[17] in old Havana. The revolution came and brought with it job security. I began filling responsible positions such as section chief in a clothing factory, union posts, and other jobs. Then I began studying, even though I had nothing more than a humble fifth grade education, and finally, I was named to the position I now hold. I think of my life as one of practical experience offset by my studies which the revolution made possible."

"Are you married?"

"I was widowed in 1961. My first husband left me with two small children in 1955. I belonged to the 26th of July Movement [a clandestine organization directed by Fidel Castro in his struggle against Batista]. The life my clandestine activity forced me to lead brought my husband and me into conflict. He tried to impose his machismo and pressure me into abandoning the struggle. For a while we fought every day. Then one day he walked out and never gave another thought to his children. I didn't miss him at all. I brought my children up by myself.

"My work in the 26th of July consisted of selling bonds to raise money, collecting medicine, clothes, carrying messages...all for the rebel army that was fighting in the mountains. That was when I started working with Erasmo, and well, we fell in love and lived together. He died fighting in the clean-up of the Escambray.[18] We had thought to marry when he came back. I don't know how to describe our relationship; perhaps full of danger. We lived those years with great intensity and comraderie...I don't know...I never fell in love again."

"How many hours do you work a day?"

"Theoretically from eight to five, but I'm practically always here."

"How do you keep up with your housework?"

"I live close by, like all the women workers, and there's not much to be done at home. It's just me and Mama. My children seldom visit.

My son is a doctor and is lending his services to Jamaica for a year. My daughter runs a high school on the Island of Youth. She got very excited about teaching when she worked in the literacy program. Even though Mama's very old, she can take care of herself. The apartment is on the ground floor, so she doesn't have to climb the stairs. She sweeps the house seven times a day because that number has a religious significance," Paulina says with a smile.

"Living in Alamar is very comfortable. Your whole life could unfold there without your ever having to go out for anything. There are movies, social and daycare centers, a medical clinic, primary and secondary schools, a market, just about everything.

"At night I cook for the next day, and Mama washes dishes for me, although she always breaks something because of the way her hands tremble. I think it's only human to leave something for old people to do. That way they feel useful. I tell her I don't know how I'll get on the day I lose her. This makes her feel good, and what's more, it's true, I'm going to feel very alone." She sighs. "I need a couple of grandchildren. My brothers and their children visit us on Sundays, but so many people around makes Mama nervous."

A young woman brings us tea. Paulina sends her off to call Nélida García and Carmona, women's union representative, and general secretary, respectively.

THE UNION

"There are 38 men and 572 women working here," Carmona explains.

"And how did they elect you when there are so many women working here?"

"I'm innocent. It's the women's fault. Why don't you ask them? It was probably because I'm so ugly," he responds jokingly, rocking back and forth in his butterball of a body.

In my opinion," Nélida says, "he's the most qualified. He's an old fighter who cares very much about all of us and the factory. Personally, I don't think that's the only reason they elected him." And teasingly, "It was for other reasons, but what Carmona says is true. You should ask around."

"But don't you think it's a concession? There had to be women, perhaps without as much experience, but nevertheless women, capable of doing the job."

"Concession? To whom?" Nélida comes back. "We don't believe we should elect women for the sake of electing women. We're not waging a war against men. Ours is a class struggle against social injustice."

"Let me give you some figures, compañera," Carmona chimes in. "Thirty percent of the Cuban workforce consists of women, yet they represent forty percent of union membership. How does that grab you?"

"Hey, Sylvia," Paulina says to the woman collecting empty tea cups, "you voted for Carmona, didn't you? Why did you vote for him and not for one of the women?"

"Because— Give me a break," she says, annoyed. "I thought he'd be better because he's a man. A man can always command more respect, right? There's a better guarantee—"

"That is a classic answer from a neophyte worker," Paulina explains. "They were housewives up until yesterday, and they still have greater respect for men as men."

"Here you have three types of working women," Paulina continues. "There's the one who's been working for years, has a class-consciousness, is disciplined and zealous in her work. There's the young woman who for some reason has not wanted to continue her studies and becomes an apprentice in our training center until she is qualified enough to begin working. And there's the older woman who up until she comes here to work has only been a housewife. The latter finds it the most difficult to adjust. She's traumatized when she sees that it is impossible to keep her house as well as before. It is difficult for her to understand that she shouldn't miss work over having the wash or shopping or something along those lines to do. Others have problems with husbands who aren't used to helping out around the house, becoming so resentful they'd prefer having less money if only their women would stay home and attend to her obligations."

"We have to give those kind of workers a lot of support," Nélida says, "so that they can bear the pressure they feel at the beginning. We have to be patient with their frequent absences and appeal to their growing worker's consciousness."

"The union," Carmona interjects, "keeps track of each worker, particularly those who are having problems. If we notice that one of them is absent a lot, fights with the others, can't get work out fast enough, or has frequent problems with her machine, Nélida goes to her and asks if she'd like to talk about it. What comes out are always personal problems which are very hard to resolve."

"What they really need," Nélida continues, "is someone they can talk to, to know that they can ask my advice...or cry if that's what they need, if it makes them feel better. Wherever there are women, there is always crying. It's very important that they shouldn't feel alone. I listen to what's hurting them. All this is part of my union work. And we do succeed in making their attitudes toward production more positive. In addition, we make them understand that they're needed and that in spite of their problems they ought to work as much as they can."

"What kind of problems come up with regard to children?"

"There are problems, but not over daycare capacity," Nélida responds, pointing toward the window. "That's big enough for all the children of all the workers in Alamar. Problems come up on the day when you'd least expect them. A mother takes her child to the center and discovers that Public Health has shut the place down because the septic tank overflowed; or there's no water because the electric pump broke down; or something breaks in the kitchen; or there's not enough oil to light the stoves, so there's no food, and so on. Then the factory turns into a chaos, an appreciable number of women don't come to work at all, and our production drops tremendously. None of this is the fault of the mothers, of course. Children getting sick is another big problem. Until the Family Code is rigorously enforced, we will continue to have mothers absent. We've got to win this battle against the men so that they share work absences when children are sick," she concludes seriously.

"Something else we've got to fight for," Carmona says, "is freeing women from working on Saturdays. All the housework piles up during the week, and if the women don't get it done on Saturday, they can't go to the beach Sunday, or wherever it is they want to go..."

"What are your prospective plans for the factory?"

"We're studying the addition of another shift in order to give work to approximately two hundred more women," Paulina explains.

"This idea came out of the Federation's Third Congress, in which Fidel proposed measures of this kind reduce the unemployment caused by the reorganization of state agencies."

"Do you know why the reorganization is being carried out?"

"Well, it's the result of the new policies, which are being implemented as our economic development demands it. Adding a shift to the work force already available in the textile industry seems right to me, if you take into consideration the enormous amount of fabric the giant Santa Clara plant is already producing."[19]

"During its Third Congress the Federation of Cuban Women set guidelines for the hiring of these new workers," Carmona says. "Management should consult the Federation before hiring so that the jobs can be given to those who need them most. If two applicants are equally qualified, the job should go to the woman with family income problems."

"That is an important clarification," Paulina says, "because despite the laws, there is discrimination against women. Now management will be penalized."

"What form does this discrimination take?"

"Well, in reserving for women jobs that allow them to remain fettered to their responsibilities at home. . . Among graduates, men are preferred. Sometimes women who have learned their work on the job are not promoted, and men are brought in to fill the higher positions. Men are also preferred for on-the-job training courses because they don't have the 'logical' limitations that women have. And so on and on. That isn't the end of it. This has got to stop. We've got to be on guard."

A long whistle is heard, and the sewing machines stop. A human river rushes into the street. "Those are the women who live nearby, and they take advantage of their lunch break to see how things are going at home." The rest of the workers calmly file into the cafeteria to get a tray of fried fish, rice, split peas, salad, orange slices in syrup, and a glass of milk. Some complain about the fish, others about the split peas, but everyone eats. The cafeteria is big and comfortable. The counters are covered with stainless steel and the dining tables with formica. The women who serve the food are all dressed in white and wear cloth masks over their mouths. The cost of the meal is nominal, only fifty centavos.

After lunch some people talk, tidy up, or relax. The rest go right back to the machines in hopes of receiving extra pay for turning out more work than is set in the guidelines.

A DISGUSTED WORKER

"I'm going to show you an interesting case," Paulina promises, "in which we weren't able to produce a favorable change in attitude. It's the case of a housewife who started working here two years ago. She's a bad example for the collective, and if she doesn't improve, I'll have to let her go, although I wouldn't feel good about it."

Betty is short, with a curvaceous figure, and her hair is dyed bright red. She would be much prettier if there were less bitterness in her expression. She looks us up and down without paying attention to the school uniforms she is handling mechanically. Her tiny fingers are inspecting the stitches in the blouses, and she is bored.

"The only thing I like less than this factory is being a quality inspector." She speaks rapidly and nervously, barely leaving room for questions, but never stopping the matching and measuring of the different blouses she stacks one on top of the other. "It's ruining my nerves to be sitting here checking and rechecking these clothes. This environment does not interest me."

"What's wrong with the environment?"

"Look, the cultural and educational level is very low and nobody ever talks about anything interesting. It's all what if the factory this, what if the policies that, what if problems at home. I aspire to other things. I feel like my mind and body are atrophying here.

"I've had problems with the management because Paulina is a very demanding black lady and Nélida nevertheless goes around trying to solve problems for the poor fools who don't know how to take care of themselves. I'm not one of those," she adds aggressively. "I know how to take care of myself, and I want change, not advice. I like to rub elbows with cultured people, because a person without culture is like a person without legs, he'll never get anywhere. I read a lot...romantic novels mostly."

"Why don't you study so that you can change jobs?"

"I don't want to study. I want to live. I'm in the middle of a divorce, and I have two children to raise. I decided to get a divorce after fifteen years of boredom, and you know what my mother says to me? She says I'm crazy for leaving a good man who brings home his salary, and that's why he's good! As far as I'm concerned there are no good men."

"Then why did you get married?"

"It was the custom. Like all women I wanted to get married. He was the first to propose. But he turned out to be a real dud, dry and boring, night after night in front of the tube, and when 'the hour of truth' came, all he thought of was his own pleasure. I want to have fun, I've got a real zest for life. I arrange *quinces*[20] to earn money and have fun with my little girls. They're all that matters to me. We have a very good relationship. As a father, he's very good, but as a husband...Now he comes up with this bit about me needing a psychiatrist, so I tell him he's the one who really needs it. Boy, does that get him! But the biggest donnybrook's gonna be when we sign the divorce papers and then go on seeing each other's face in the same house, because he doesn't have anywhere else to go, and I don't either.

"Lately, I don't know what's got into him. He's making my life impossible. He watches me...says any man on the street could fool me. You think that with all the advances women have made today anybody could fool us? What he doesn't know," she says doubling over in laughter, "is that I've got a twenty-seven-year-old boyfriend with big green eyes..."

The woman sharing the table with Betty has been following the conversation and argues that Betty "speaks for herself," that the factory is a good place to work where women can do tasks that are "appropriate" for them. "For older housewives like me, who haven't any skills or work experience, the factory gives us an opportunity to feel useful and earn a salary. I got bored at home because my children are married and don't live with us. What am I supposed to do, stay home alone all day? I think about sickness, imagine that it hurts me here, or hurts me there...and my husband doesn't get home until nighttime. Now I don't have to report every penny I spend, and that is really wonderful, isn't it?"

Paulina is worried because she didn't have time on her lunch hour to go home and see how her mother is doing. The sun gives off endless light and makes the two blocks home to Paulina's five-story modern apartment building even longer. In the doorway, rocking herself back and forth in a rocking chair, we find her.

MARIA CARIDAD

"I don't know what day I was born, but I haven't forgotten the year, it was in 1899...I'm going to be eighty-one."

She is black, very wrinkled, with her gaze lost at sea. A delicate but vital energy comes from her friendly expression and soft, kindly smile. Her hair and the long whiskers growing on her chin are very white. The kerchief around her head is white, as are her long dress, stockings, and slippers. She is adorned with a string of colored beads strung seven by seven. (Seven of one color, then seven of the next, and so on, the colors pertaining to specific "saints" or gods and identify her as a "child" or devotee of that "saint" as well as protecting her. The number seven, of course, has some specific meaning.) Gold rings dangle from her ears.

Maria Caridad's entire outfit corresponds to the features of her African religion. Between her bony fingers she holds a dead cigar, fat and black, which she later places behind her left ear; behind her right ear is a sprig of fragrant broom, which, infused in alcohol, is used for friction baths and for "banishing spirits and curses."

"My Tomas was very handsome...he died in 1954...I didn't get together with anyone after that because I didn't find another I liked.

"There are so many things I can't remember! I went to work on October 14, 1911. I was still a little girl. It was in the tobacco plant of a Spaniard, a hard man who yelled a lot, but who wasn't bad at heart...Stemming was the worst job. That's why they gave it to us black women. I earned about five pesos a week; the women who rolled earned more but they were all white, and the even better jobs were given to the men...especially slicing. If the owner found a little bit of tobacco leaf left on one of my stems, I'd be back on the street in no time...We worked very hard for four months until December, because the international demand was very high...but then there was no more stemming to do, and we were left to our misery...At that time I lived in Las Yaguas.[21]

"Las Yaguas...hmmmm. Everything there was little curvy streets. The streets wasn't streets really. It was just alleyways and alleyways.

Yeah, yeah, there was lots of crooks around, but lots of them were not from Las Yaguas...they used to steal my electricity, because I know they did...And it wasn't like I wanted to have a big dream house or nothin', just four walls...There was always tremendous fights going on, because there were good ones and there were bad ones, because in Las Yaguas there are a lots of tramps"—because of her age Maria confuses the past and the present—"thieves that fall in with the people that is already there and smoke lots of marijuana...but then they don't come from Las Yaguas either and misery loves company, ha, ha, ha, ha! Of course! People came from Matanzas. That's inconceivable today because you go to a train station and can't buy a ticket to leave the same day, you have to buy it ahead of time...What a place it was! All the houses was made out of what people throwed away, and they was so close together they looked like one house...There were thousands of us...The neighbors always went round tearing down Coca-Cola and Pepsi Cola signs to patch up the holes in their roofs.

"In 1930 I got some kind of facial paralysis and Doctor Suárez Pupo...this was all so long ago!...told me, O.K., you're gonna be like this for another year or two and won't be able to work. I couldn't chew. Juice and milk was all right, but chewing was out. Afterward, with some electric thing and a few injections I started getting better, but when I went back to work they didn't want me because I was still funny-looking and weak. I did the cat-on-her-back routine for the owner until he felt sorry for me and let me stay. Tears always soften the men..." She laughs, puts the cigar to her lips, and bites on it.

"I'm too old to do anything now. In 1935 we all got carried away with the strike. The crowd was really wild! The police caught me carrying a sign demanding a salary hike and an eight-hour day. They beat me like a drum, who knows why, and took me prisoner...We worked till we dropped, even Sundays; I was just a little girl...They let me go after a few days. I have a lot of luck and am protected...A lot of people are protected by the Virgen del Caridad del Cobre. She helps a lot, you see...I had eight children and all of them came out all right. Paulina was born on the Calle Merced during the cyclone of 1926. I sold all my furniture and everything. I sold it on the Calle Salud; that's where things were bought and sold, beautiful, good things...My brother was killed on the Calle Merced."

"Who killed him?"

"I don't know any more than you do! There was so much killing going on that anyone could turn up dead on the street. All I know is that he was found like all the other dead, just dumped somewhere... Don't you remember how the rich were sending their children away back in Batista's time? Don't you believe me? But they did, Child. You must know that this is the way things were. They were afraid something would happen to their children if they stayed in Cuba...I used to have papers from those days that told about this; I kept them in a box, and one day my house caught fire and burned almost all of them. But so help me, a neighbor woman put it out with a hose, because if she hadn't..." Her curved fingers light up the cigar.

"How long have you been smoking?"

"I smoke because my father taught me how, and after that I smoked more, when I stemmed tobacco. Now I have to restrain myself because it's very expensive. I light up and then let it go out. Then I light up again, so that it smoulders and lasts me longer. How barbaric, people today saying tobacco gives you cancer. It's a lie, Child; I'm telling you this as someone who's spent her life between tobacco leaves...Craziness, yes, but not cancer, you see? I've seen tons of smokers go crazy."

"Do you believe in spirits?"

"You have to believe in the dead...The universe is no simple place, and there are people with the evil eye. Look, not long ago I was lying down...thinking with my eyes wide open, waiting for my daughter Paulina; and wouldn't you know but I start to feel snow falling, fine, very fine snow drowning me, and I started praying to my guardian angel, who is Blessed Santa Barbara on the spiritual level. Suddenly I saw the warrior, Siete Rayos, who appears in the form of a woman as often as in that of a man, come riding in on his horse, Palo Monte. So I said, 'Kabio Kabiosile Shango!' As soon as he came in to throw that lightning bolt, all the coldness began to melt away...until finally I could get up and turn on the light...and wouldn't you know, I wasn't wet at all. I don't even want to think about it. The next morning I made him a really nice offering...with ripe bananas."

"How did your husband court you?"

"You sure is nosy! All right, when I was young, if a man wanted to court a girl, first the girl's father, her mother, and all the rest of the family, the entire family, would have to like him. After that, they'd give him the go-ahead, and he could come visit two or three times a week at certain fixed hours...It was very beautiful...The boyfriend would always bring a box of sweets to please everybody...little horses made of cake and toasted peanuts...You don't see that anymore. The grandmother would watch the couple, and if she fell asleep they would kiss. There were girls who didn't marry until ten or twelve years later...The men would get tired of this, but that's how things were done...It was always the same, there was no money in those days, it was bad business."

"When did you stop working?"

"As soon as Fidel was in, right then and there I asked for retirement! I'd been worked to the bone and then there were all these speeches, guns, problems, pushing and pulling, this way and that. I got nervous and shut myself in the house for some peace and quiet...then Paulinita moved in with me, it's boring here, too much countryside and no dancing..."

"Don't you like Fidel?"

"I respect poor Fidel, because he's noble, noooo...It's true he's a noble man, mm-hmm, I know him, and even though you don't, I'll tell you something. Here, in Cuba, never ever this?" She points to her black skin. "Help this? Ha, ha, ha, ha. The truth! It's the truth! There has never been a president that cared, no, no, noooo. They've got it all, the aristocracy, living and owning, but the black man? One of our children in school? O.K., there were schools, but you know very well that classes at the normal school cost money! And the high school? The big thick books? They cost money. No poor person around here could afford that...Mothers like me had to take in more wash, wash, and wash until they dissolved, or work like mules for...you know? I'm not lying! All over the Republic, right this very moment, from the mountains inland, not just here, from the mountains inland, they're opening schools. It's the truth!" Putting two fingers to her forehead, "How much does it cost? Those who aren't day students get full room and board...But around here the only scholarships were the ones given out by the Beneficencia[22]...I had to pay Dr. Portela for my children because he was the school's director. I'm going to show you the receipt so you'll see, fifteen pesos for Paulinita! And fifteen more for José Tómas! And this is what they called 'free.' But if you didn't pay, the kid couldn't go to school, and then you'd have to go find a politician; hand over the I.D. so that the kid could stay in school a bit longer. In order to avoid having to do that, I paid! Then I got myself a recommendation from a mulatto from Santiago de Cuba who was later on Batista's Advisory Commission. I went for about two years without paying a cent. That's how I saved money. The Beneficencia...was for orphans only. I paid for mine...so don't go thinking everything that glitters is gold, because there are a lot of things that are 'prettied up' and only the ones who are in on it know...Like this Fidel...there's no other, the blacks of Africa and of everywhere...all over the world on their knees asking for mercy to serve Christ, because, listen, I'm telling you, I've never done a thing, and if this thing [the Revolution] fails, they'll cut off my head; and around here that would have very bad consequences, yes, because they figure...O.K., there are a lot of black women who they gave houses to that live as they've never lived before, it's the truth. And later all of them would pay for what happened to me. Off with their heads! So I start with myself praying for mercy, that divine white banner, no, no, nooo, because in every case it would come to no good, houses destroyed, because as soon as the first missile is fired, Cuba is finished! There's something wrong here...A few days ago Fidel came on the radio and said that there was a crisis, an international crisis and a crisis here in Cuba. It seems that he smelled something funny, he said it about three times, there is a crisis, and we have to be...there is a big crisis...there are 1630 persons who have taken refuge there[23] and outside there are hordes more, and if Peru is going to take them to their Peru, let her take them! Why don't those people bring boats and airplanes and take them all away?"

"When do you go out?"

"In the morning I take a little walk looking for dandelions, cress, and other herbs for remedies...when the sun is low. Nature can cure everything. I go to market to buy my tobacco and talk to the old women. I've always been very popular and have helped a lot of humanity, for nothing, 'cuz I hardly ever get thanked; I do it on a celestial commission...I know all the curative herbs. Where I place my hand, sickness disappears. There was a lot of misery where I used to live, and nobody could afford a doctor...

"Around the house? I don't do much. I've seen too much suffering and humiliation in my day...People have to learn to do good things for themselves in order to go on. I'll never quit praying."

"Do you like television?"

"It bothers my eyes, Child."

Clouds hinting of rain come floating in from the sea. Maria Caridad's mood is a overcast as the sky. We say goodbye in a hurry in order to catch the bus.

"Don't worry about a thing, Child," she says solemnly, raising her vein-lined arms to the sky:

"San Isidro, the tillerman,
lift the water and bring the sun.

"I'm going to make a cross with ashes right now, and then you'll see!"

"The black contribution to Cuba has not been slight. Apart from the immense work force which made Cuba's economic incorporation into world-wide civilization possible...African cultural influence is felt in the choice of foodstuffs, the cooking, the vocabulary, the romantic character, the art, the religion, and the emotive tone of the collective. In art, music belongs to the blacks. The extraordinary vigor and captivating originality of Cuban music is a creole (a cross of black and white) creation...today, *habañeras*, *danzones*, *sones*, and *rumbas*, Afrocuban music, which is to say, creole music, is danced the world over. The power of the creole *conga* sweeps the crowds into a joyful and anesthetizing release of their neurotic anguish.

"In religion, the black man, distrusting the foreign and colonial clergy which kept him in slavery and exploited him, compared his myths with those of the whites and so created for the great mass of our people a syncretic system of equivalents....the black man's inherent culture and soul, always in transitional crisis, penetrate Cuba through a mixing of bloods and cultures, soaking Cuba in the juicy, sensual, happy-go-lucky, tolerant, accommodating and witty character which is its charm, its magic and its most potent means of resistence for survival in the constant stewing of the unsavory that has been the history of this country."

FERNANDO ORTIZ 1881-1969
Cuban scholar, anthropologist, ethnographer,
folklorist, and lexicographer

More women than men work in the Cuban textile factories. JØRGEN SCHYTTE

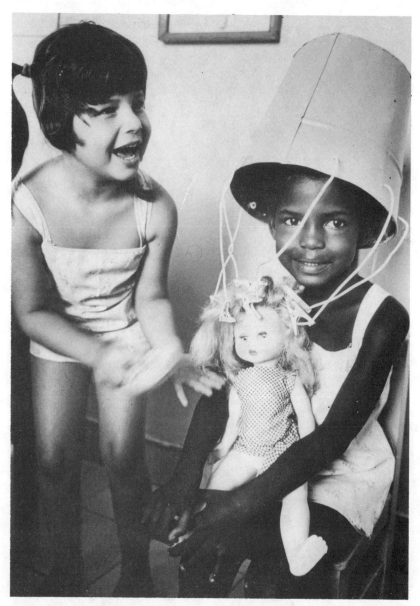

At play in a daycare center for working mothers. JØRGEN SCHYTTE

Students at secondary schools located in the countryside work three hours a day at agricultural tasks. JØRGEN SCHYTTE

Students teachers gain practice in the daycare centers provided for working women. JØRGEN SCHYTTE

Children's health care is carefully supervised, with needed shots, medications, and checkups given regularly.
Jørgen Schytte

Macheteros *like this man come from the city to work voluntarily in the cane-cutting season.* Inger Holt-Seeland

A country kitchen with a kerosene stove up in the mountains. INGER HOLT-SEELAND·

THE WOMAN IN CUBA
A Synthesis of History, Geography, and Contemporary Politics

GEOGRAPHY

What everyone knows as the island of Cuba is in reality a verdant archipelago of some 10,922 square kilometers. The Isle of Pines—now called the Island of Youth—where "the skies are covered with reddish mists," as Alexander Humbolt reported it in 1840, covers some 2,200 square kilometers, and the chain of keys or little islands that surrounds it accounts for 3,715 square kilometers.

The country's complex and diverse topography includes eastern, central, and western mountain ranges. The highest elevation is 2,000 meters at Peak Turquino, and the lowest point is 7,243 meters below sea level in the Oriente Trench. Countless beaches adorn the coast.

Because of Cuba's tropical climate, which is influenced by the Gulf Stream, the coastal waters vary only between 26° and 30° C. year

round. There are rainstorms twelve months out of the year. Daytime
relative humidity is 60 percent, rising to 80 percent at night. The mean
annual temperature is 25.5° C: the coldest month of the year is January, with an average of 22.5° C, and the warmest month is August,
when the mean temperature is 27.8° C.

There are few large rivers in Cuba. The Cuban soil is fertile and
rich in minerals such as iron, copper, and nickel. The forests exhausted
by indiscriminent exploitation are being restored with the planting of
more than 600 million trees.

Agriculture and Industry. Before 1959 the country's agriculture was
based on three principal crops: sugar, coffee, and tobacco. Today,
although sugar cane retains its importance, Cuba's agriculture is being
diversified through the production of citrus fruits, other fruits and
vegetables, rice, and cattle.

Industrial development is directed toward the food, metalurgical,
chemical, and petrochemical industries, with emphasis on the production of fertilizers, agricultural machinery, building and construction materials for new housing, towns, roads, irrigation, and so on.

The fishing industry and the merchant marine deserve special
mention. Thanks to the island's geographical position, Cuban ships
have easy access to the Atlantic Ocean's most bountiful waters. Cuba
now holds first place among all of of Latin American in the growth
rate in these categories.

Transportation. The country has good road, air, and railroad transportation to all of its regions.

Population. The 1974 census shows that the Cuban population has
risen to 9.3 million whites, blacks, and mulattos. Of that total, 4.3
million are women. The annual rate of population growth is 1.65 percent.

Political-Administrative Division. When the Revolution came to power,
Cuba's administrative-political division had not changed since the
colonial Spanish government established six provinces and 132 municipalities in 1878. Today there are fourteen provinces and one special municipality, the Island of Youth. The provinces contain 169
municipalities.

Language. Hispanic cultural influence continues to predominate
in Cuba. Although Spanish is the official language, Cubans have
many unique speech characteristics and habits which allow Hispanic,
African, and Chinese influences to fuse into a single cultural identity
that asserts itself through a myriad artistic and cultural forms.

*"That great heart which shows itself
in great things."*

—CHRISTOPHER COLUMBUS

HISTORY

Discovery. Floating flowers and flocks of birds were the harbingers. On watch from the crow's next, at daybreak on the twelfth of October, 1492, Rodrigo Berguemo, a native of Triana, cried, "Laaaaaaaaand!" It was the first European contact "with the most beautiful land..."

Sixteen days later, his eyes weary from the sun and the sea, Columbus dressed in his Sunday best before setting foot on the island of Cuba, hoping he had found the kingdom of the Great Kahn. He sent forth ambassadors, one of whom was well versed in Hebrew, Chaldean and even "Arabig"; but instead of the Kahn, they found only an immense green forest, a single shadow spreading under a canopy of vegetation, incredible birds, the perfume of strange flowers, "fruits of marvelous flavor...sweet and delicious air," and one small village of fifty houses where they were solemnly greeted by a naked, innocent, and beautiful people whom they called Indians.

The First Cuban Women. At the time of the discovery Indian women had no problems of social equality with men. Indian society was matriarchal, "which is to say, a society administered and directed by the ideas and will of a woman, of which the most typical example was the tribe governed by Anacaona in Santo Domingo, after her brother Caonabo was killed in a treacherous ambush."[24]

The island's colonization and the genocide of its original inhabitants completed, the Spaniards began to import blacks from Africa through the institution of slavery.

In need of women—the instruments of labor, sex, and reproduction—the importation of black women was increased considerably. In the year 1859 alone, 30,473 blacks entered Cuba. White women were extremely scarce.

"Although the conquest and colonization of Cuba took place well into the sixteenth century, when a few European states such as France and England had already begun the process of capitalistic development, the regime Spain founded in our country was one in which aspects of nascent capitalism were quickly coupled with feudalism and slavery."[25]

It was in this setting that free white women—Spanish and creole—black and Indian slavewomen alike were subjected to total dependence on men as sanctioned by the Catholic Church. Cuban women could not legally own property. As an example of Caribbean women's situation in general at that time, on the neighboring island of Santo Domingo prostitution came under government regulation.

The Struggle for Independence. Between 1868 and 1878 Cuban men and women—"we can speak of war in front of our women," as Martí said—tried to gain independence from Spain, but their attempt failed.

One high-ranking Spanish military official attributed the perseverance of Cubans fighting in the countryside to the influence exercised by the women's unwavering patriotism.

During this war, which was called the Ten Year War, and before the Guaimaro Assembly, a Cuban woman, Anna Betancourt, became the first woman in the American setting to plead for civil rights for women. She was an exceptional Cuban, and she suffered imprisonment and exile.

In 1895 the conflict recommenced, and in 1898 Cubans gained the victory that put an end to four hundred years of Spanish domination.

When the war was nearly over, the United States joined in, and succeeded in getting Cuba to fall into its colonial sphere.

In 1898, military government by the United States was begun in Cuba, and it would last until 1902.

The Republic. From 1902 to 1934 Cuba was governed under a constitution containing an ominous proviso known as the Platt Amendment. It guaranteed that Cuba would be dependent on the United States.

Paradoxically, this constitutional proviso prohibited Cuba from making treaties or pacts that would "compromise Cuban sovereignty or involve the cession of territory"; it prohibited Cuba from contracting debts beyond her capacity to redeem the same; and it gave to the United States the right to intervene militarily on Cuban soil according to its interests, occupying parts of its territory with naval bases. The United States naval base at Guantanamo Bay, which still exists, is a consequence of the Platt Amendment.

In 1903 the North Americans imposed the Treaty of Commercial Reciprocity on Cuba to assure control over Cuban markets and to convert Cuba into its own low-cost sugar and tobacco producer.

In accordance with what was set down in the Platt Amendment, the United States intervened and occupied Cuba in 1906, 1912, 1917, and 1920, and after 1933, when the people rose up against the Machado dictatorship, an American Navy flotilla was permanently stationed off the coast of Cuba.

That same year Fulgencio Batista staged his coup d'etat and seized power, and he remained in control until 1944, with a few intermissions. In 1952 Batista again took power by the same means.

In 1934 the United States imposed the signing of yet another Commercial Reciprocity Treaty to replace the treaty of 1905. The new treaty increased American exports to Cuba and asserted United States domination of the sugar market and the Cuban economy.

As a result of this dependence on the United States Cuba suffered destructive governments, without exception, from 1902 to 1959, when Fidel Castro at last overthrew the Batista dictatorship.

Closely related events prevented the country from developing a healthy infrastructure, which was indispensable to its economic development, and relegated Cuba to the miserable role of consumer and exporter of nothing but sugar and tobacco, products dependent on the artificial ups and downs of the international market.

Cuba, a predominantly agricultural country, managed to import from Miami on a daily basis the vegetables consumed in the capital.

The penetration of foreign capital, principally North American, is illustrated by the following: "Out of approximately 31 million sacks of sugar harvested in 1926-27, 19.5 million were refined in American mills, this is 62.5 percent. . . . Americn firms and individuals rented or owned at least 5,740,000 acres or 22 percent of Cuba's total area."[26]

This great expansion of the sugar industry came at the expense of thousands of peasant families forcibly removed from their homes without prior notice, left completely helpless, their houses burned, and many of those who protested, murdered.

Cuba's proximity to the United States deprived the country of stores, factories, and industries, and the inevitable consequence was endemic unemployment. Four hundred thousand families were residing in shanty towns; 90 percent of the rural child population was infected with parasites; and there were almost no medical attention, hospitals, or schools. There was approximately one physician for every thousand inhabitants and 65 percent were based in Havana, and the rest were in the major cities and towns.

The present tourist area around the Bay of Pigs—a considerable expanse comprising hundreds of square miles and bordered by swampland—was once inhabited only by mosquito-eaten workers who gathered wood from the mire to make into charcoal. There wasn't a trace of civilization: no roads, no schools, no electricity. The sick from this area were taken to the coast where they sent up smoke signals with bonfires in hopes of attracting the attention of some little boat that might stop and carry them back to civilization. Rough-hewn wooden crosses are silent testimony to those who died there without hope. Similar dramas were enacted in Baracoa and other isolated regions of Cuba.

Nevertheless, Cuba was a country of millionaires . . . and beggars. Havana was known as "the Paris of America." It was a fun city, the city of lights, ready to entertain tourists and sailors in search of Chanel No. 5, alligator ware, Dirty Dick's Bar, Sloppy Joe's Bar, an abortion, Hemingway, and the daiquiris of the Floridita.

The shadow of "the Godfather" also slank along the walls of luxurious hotels and casinos. There were neighborhoods filled with prostitutes and pimps; pornography, contraband, and drugs; and poverty-stricken children, begging, shining shoes, and steering clients to brothels.

This was a country ruled by dictators and by democratic administrations so representative of a people that the cost of getting rid of them was twenty thousand lives.

In 1924, Don Fernando Ortiz, the scholar we have mentioned before, offered frightening data at a conference he called "The Cuban Decadence":

"In Cuba 53 percent of the population is illiterate; more than 50 percent of school-age children do not go to school; in the past fifteen years illiteracy has risen 15 percent for young whites and 22 percent for young blacks; out of every hundred students, not one completes elementary school; the figure is one out of 215; 20 percent of all political candidates nominated in 1922 had criminal records; the suicide rate is seven times what it was twenty-two years ago."

The goal of politicians was to complete their terms with their pockets full. You could see them cruising the streets in the latest model American cars even before those cars could be seen in the United States. The peso was exchanged at par with the dollar, and this permitted the Cuban aristocracy to obtain exclusive Dior clothes in the department store called El Encanto.

It was the store for "high society," where it could happen that a lady would be waited on by her honorable husband's mistress, whose jewels would rival her own, where mistresses and wives bought jewels in competition with one another. It was the only place in Cuba where some of the salesgirls, alumnae of the Catholic high school run by the Oblata Order, were black, a fact with which the aristocracy neatly tried to belie the reality of racial discrimination.

The girls hired for El Encanto were chosen for their beauty and manners. They were much sought after once their pictures appeared in that notorious "photo album" of Marina's—Havana's infamous and wealthy madam—in which clients could select a companion for an "unforgettable evening."

All this occurred even after the Constitution of 1940, a great step forward, had already been proclaimed. It wasn't until the Second World War was in full swing, and progressive and antifascist forces were united, that it was suggested a law should be passed giving women and blacks the same rights as white men, along with equal pay for equal work, and equal opportunity for all, regardless of sex or race. This law was never passed.

It is interesting to note that Cuban women did not win the suffrage until 1935, fifteen years after it was established in the United States.

On the 26th of July in 1953, Fidel Castro led a group of young men in an attack on the Moncada Barracks in Santiago de Cuba, but Batista's forces were the victors in the ensuing bloodbath. Imprisoned at first, but later released because of popular pressure, Fidel Castro and the other youths who survived at Moncada emigrated to Mexico. There they organized and trained under the direction of General Bayo, a veteran of the Spanish War.

On December 2, 1956, Fidel Castro and 82 other soldiers sailed in a tiny cabin cruiser called the *Granma* and landed in Cuba's Oriente province, close to the Sierra Maestra.

Only twelve of these men survived the landing. They began guerrilla warfare in the mountains, with the support of clandestine movements in the cities, that continued until revolutionary triumph on the first day of January, 1959.

The Revolution. With the firm support of the people, the Revolution gave impetus to a total transformation of the country.

On the second of December, 1960, more than a million Cubans

gathered for a General National Assembly in the Plaza de la Revolución, where they condemned the inequality and exploitation of women, and granted to women social, civil, and political equality. The document resulting from this condemnation is known as the First Declaration of Havana. It recognizes woman's role in Cuban struggles throughout history, for she was present in the war against Spain, present in the struggle against the pseudo republic, present at the Moncada.

Many measures designed to benefit the populace were put into effect at this time.

New jobs were created, salaries were raised, rents were lowered. The cost of electricity, medicine, and other common expenditures was reduced.

In 1959 a law was passed based on the principle that land should belong to the person who works it, that no one should possess land he himself does not cultivate, that no one had the right to ask a peasant to pay rent on a piece of land the latter was cultivating, and other measures.

Foreign and Cuban companies owning great amounts of land opposed the agrarian reform bill, and relations with the United States deteriorated even further, and aggressive actions of every kind ensued.

The United States cut off purchases of Cuban sugar, and the oil companies threatened to leave the country without an oil supply.

The Soviet Union decided to help Cuba by purchasing the sugar previously bought by the United States, and it began to supply the oil that the country needed.

In January of 1961 the United States withdrew its diplomatic and consular representation and went on to outright armed aggression and an economic blockade. From then to now, diplomatic relations have not substantially improved.

Religion. Cuba's major religion, Catholicism, was introduced by the Spanish colonizers.

Until 1959 the Church relied on the support of the state and aristocratic classes. It was, until 1959, a predominant force in politics and business. It controlled immense capital through its holdings of real estate, newspapers, cemetaries, and other properties.

The Catholic Church opposed the revolutionary process from the beginning, organizing conspiracies of various kinds to sabotage the fledgling communist state. The Church's opposition was due, among other factors, to the new laws that affected its wealth.

Nevertheless, the government maintained a moderate position and didn't encourage antireligious campaigns, nor did it suggest measures be taken against the Church.

It is well known that the churches lost most of their members after 1959: the upper bourgeoisie abandoned the country, and most of the faithful who remained in Cuba have joined the Revolution. Being religious does not preclude joining the people's organizations, but it is limiting for anyone wishing to become a member of the Communist Party.

As of late the Cuban churches have assumed a conciliatory attitude. The official stance is acceptance of the revolutionary process, and clerical participation in volunteer work is not uncommon.

The Catholic Church's newest policy is designed to regain lost ground by creating an environment attractive to youth with contemporary music, movies, conferences on sexuality, parties, and other activities.

Culture. Although the people are the legitimate owners of culture, this was denied them by the dominant classes who cheapened culture's true significance and turned it into merchandise.

More than a million could not read a book because of illiteracy, and millions more could not afford even to buy a book.

The ruling classes, particularly the nouveau riche, left evidence of their lack of culture in enormous palaces stuffed with pompous bad taste. It was not unusual to find ostentatious personal libraries of hollow books bound in leather and gold. Books were bought by the meter, color, and size to fill the shelves of some residences.

An entire generation of painters equal in stature to the extraordinary Victor Manuel went hungry, and actors would prostitute themselves for a television or theatre contract. It was a time when physical attractiveness overshadowed talent.

In the magazine *Revista Conjunto: Teatro Latinoamericano Casa de las Americas*, number 27, 1976, the Cuban writer Carlos Espinosa Domínguez wrote with great discernment: "Many years of cultural deformation of the collective dulling of our sensibility through the colonization of esthetic taste and the suppression of national culture have made it seem that the people were losing their identity, losing their awareness that they themselves are the fundamental creators of art and culture, and above all, underestimating their true creative power."

The past twenty years of the Revolution have seen a great development of culture in all its manifestations.

"With the Revolution, everything; against the Revolution, nothing" is the motto for a great freedom as regards artistic form, although not so in respect to ideological criticism. Nevertheless, constructive criticism is practiced as widely in literature as in film and theatre.

Alicia Alonso's Cuban School of Ballet is world famous. Other modern and folkloric dance troupes are also very well known.

Cultured music is sure to be interpreted by the National Symphony Orchestra as well as by individual pianists, guitar players, and other quality artists.

Numerous bands play Cuban popular music, and outstanding groups such as Irakere have achieved international recognition.

Young people's music is represented by the Nueva Trova, a group of innovative troubadors who embody the folk tradition.

These musicians, dancers, and other artists reach a wide public over numerous radio and television stations.

According to a statement issued by Alfredo Guevara, founder of the Cuban Institute of Cinematographic Art and Industry (ICAIC), Cuban film has become an instrument of decolonization insofar as it confirms the autonomy and authenticity of the individual viewer and the public in its general effect. This contributes to the development both of personal and national identity.

It can be said that Cuban film was born with the Revolution and is already world renowned for the innumerable honors it has won. Films about women have gained the best reception overseas; *Lucia, A Portrait of Teresa, Manuela*, and other films are prime examples.

The cinemobile which travels to the most isolated spots in the country, including the mountains, has allowed thousands of peasants to see movies for the first time.

The Casa de las Americas, which performs many functions in addition to concerning itself with Latin American culture in particular, has instituted the American literature contest known as the Premio Casa for a variety of literary genres. This annual competition enjoys great prestige.

The growing publishing industry, the increasing number of galleries and museums, have given to the people the means to learn about the variety and wealth of Cuban and universal culture.

Books are sold at very low prices. You can obtain any classic book or novel anywhere from fifty centavos to a peso. Sumptuously bound books are not common.

Television reaches every part of the country over three channels that transmit more than seven hours of programming a day. These hours are increased during school vacation.

The quality of the programs leaves something to be desired but the material difficulties faced in the field of television should be taken into consideration. Very recently, programs and series which will set future standards have been produced with new miniaturized equipment and other equipment for color.

Cuban theatres have varied repertoires, everything from Brecht's *Galileo Galilei*, Shakespeare, Ibsen and Grotowski, to lyric theatre, musicals, and opera.

The provincial capitals have theatre groups and theatre for children.

Theater was never know in the countryside. That is why theatre groups like Escambray and La Yaya en Matagua have sprung up. The actors who make up the corps of La Yaya en Matagua were originally peasants from Matagua who became actors "as a result of the need to find an adequate means of expression; a category of popular theatre in which the people take part without limiting themselves to the role of cultural consumer, in other words, they are giving the theatre back to the people." These are the words of Jesus Hernandez, Party Secretary in Matagua, as published in the aforementioned *Revista Conjunto*.

ORGANIZATIONS

National Assembly of Popular Power. The Cuban State, in accordance with the Constitution of 1976, is ruled by one supreme organization, the National Assembly of Popular Power, made up of 481 deputies elected directly in 169 cities for a term of three years.

The President elected by the Assembly becomes the chief of state and the head of government.

The Cuban Communist Party. Formed in 1962, the Communist Party is the only existing political party. Members are admitted after a rigorous and individual selection process which depends largely on consultation with workers.

In 1974 women represented 14 percent of the membership and 10 percent of the administration. In 1978 this grew to 19 percent and 15 percent respectively.

Union of Young Communists. This organization is one of the principal talent pools on which the Party draws. At present, more than one third of those admitted to the Party come from the Union. Forty-one percent of the "militants," or members, are women, as are 40 percent of those in the Union's administration.

Student Organizations. The Pioneers Union of Cuba, founded in 1961, has a membership of about two million children; this represented 98.7 percent of the total number of school children. Seventy-five percent of the leaders are girls.

The Middle School Student Federation's (FEEM) leadership is 66 percent women.

In 1974 women represented 34 percent of the leadership of the University Students Federation, and in 1978 that figure rose to 46 percent.

The Cuban Workers Central (CTC). The CTC is the workers's trade-union organization. It has more than two million members, of whom 30 percent are women. Women constitute 40 percent of the leadership.

One essential element of CTC work is the Women's Front. Workers at each workplace elect one woman to the Front. Her responsibilities include identifying and solving the problems that come between women workers and high productivity; arranging daycare centers and school lunches for the workers' children; visiting the women's homes to help in cases of sickness; lobbying for special hours for the women who need them; making sure the job assigned to a woman is compatible with her physical ability; arranging leaves of absence; struggling to eliminate the preferential hiring of men; fighting to reduce a woman's workload to five days a week and seven hours a day; and finally, dealing with any additional problems that affect the lot of the woman workers.

Social and people's organizations that support government action are:

National Association of Small Farmers (ANAP). This organization sprang up to continue the traditional peasant struggle on May 17, 1961, when small farmers came together. The Association plays an important role in agricultural production and therefore in the Cuban economy. Small farmers grow the bulk of the tobacco and coffee; they raise 26 percent of Cuba's cattle, 18 percent of her sugar cane; and they are responsible for more than half the fruit and vegetable harvest.

There are 232,358 Association members nationwide; of this total 162,126 are farm-owners, the rest are associated domestic workers. Nine percent of the total are women, and 8 percent of these women figure in the administration.

FMC-ANAP Brigades. There are 5,996 Brigades for mutual aid made up of members of ANAP and the Federation of Cuban Women. The membership comprises 73,346 peasant women. The objective of the Brigades is to contribute to the women's ideological and cultural development and to bring them into the salaried agricultural work force, for instance, raising domestic animals for national consumption.

The Brigades are not only involved in projects on members' family farms, they also work on state plans and granges. For instance, they participate in sugar, coffee, tobacco, and other harvests, in addition to performing volunteer work that helps to shape political consciousness.

The Revolutionary Defense Committees (CDR). The CDRs, taken together, form the largest popular organization. Its almost five million associates are known as *cederistas*.

The Committees were organized at the triumph of the Revolution (1960) to watch for and combat counterrevolutionaries. When Playa Giron was attacked, they sprang into action and paralyzed the internal operations of declared enemies.

They take on countless cultural and sports projects, diverse volunteer work, different kinds of censuses, polio vaccinations, night watches, and whatever other task they are assigned.

Committee women account for 41 percent of all members and hold 66 percent of the managerial positions. Joining a Committee is completely voluntary, and dues are not required.

The conviction and cohesion of the CDRs became evident during the events at the Peruvian Embassy in Havana.[23] On the nineteenth day of April, 1980, the CDRs organized a demonstration in front of the embassy that lasted for over thirteen hours and involved more than a million Cubans.

THE FEDERATION OF CUBAN WOMEN (FMC) AND THE ROLE OF WOMEN IN CUBAN LIFE

The FMC was founded in 1960 to bring together all existing revolutionary women's organizations—workers, pleasants, students, home-

makers, professionals and others. Eighty percent of the female population now belongs to the Federation. There are as many as 2,362,559
federadas or members. Any woman fourteen years old and over is free
to join the Federation.

The FMC watchword is the struggle for full equality for women,
and among its goals are cultural, political, ideological, and technical
excellence and their embodiment in the workplace.

The organization takes an active part in Cuban women's daily
lives and inspires them to do many tasks. The participation of 91,000
federadas in the literacy campaign was a determining factor in its
success, and the federadas' presence in skill-improvement courses,
political studies, peasant and family education, public health, solidarity among nations, agricultural, defense, sports and other projects is
equally important.

Among the rank-and-file federadas are 340,376 activists who volunteer their work, on the financial, educational, social work, friend-
ship between nations, and other fronts.

The FMC's energetic work for the International Democratic Federation of Women (FDIM) is very notable. A Cuban woman is FDIM
vice-president, and the FMC has a permanent position in the secretariat.

The Legacy of the Past. Before the Revolution prostitution was organized, and thousands of people lived off it. There were brothels in
every town of the country. Havana had the largest of them all, known
as the Barrio de Colón.

Twenty city blocks! Two million, one hundred and fifty-two thousand, seven hundred and eighty-two square feet of houses dedicated
to corruption! Right at the heart of the capital, next to the Paseo del
Prado, the National Capitol, the Parque Central, and the Presidential
Palace.

Prostitution preyed primarily on young and pretty country girls
lured to the city by pimps with false promises of work or love. The
pimps were real characters, and the police, who made more money
off the business than anyone else, protected them. It was not unusual
to see a pimp run successfully for political office.

The capital had four other neighborhoods devoted to prostitution, and entire streets were canvassed by women selling their love.

Different statistics have come out for the number of prostitutes in
Cuba. Someone has said 11,500, which is ridiculous. It is possible that
there were more than 100,000.

At the triumph of the Revolution prostitution was prohibited. The FMC took charge of rehabilitating former prostitutes and eradicating juvenile delinquency.

Juvenile delinquency was bred among the thousands of children who went barefoot and hungry in the street, begging, shining shoes, and selling newspapers.

The Working Woman. In 1958 there were 192,000 working women; today that figure has risen to 800,600. However, this increase is not as important as the change in the kinds of jobs women now hold.

In 1953 70 percent of all working women were domestic servants lacking any legal protection. Average salaries did not surpass 15 pesos. The "trade of marriage" became a natural escape route.

Between 1975 and 1980, 78,000 qualified women went to work as doctors, architects, technicians, and at other skilled trades.

In 1968 the Ministry of Labor passed various resolutions to reorganize the work force in order to guarantee a fair distribution of jobs among men and women.

An early revolutionary law that prohibits women from taking certain jobs is still in effect. The intention was to protect women from anything that might threaten their ability to bear children. At the FMC's request, the law is being revised and adapted to women's current reality.

The number of women working in construction (previously a job for men only) has risen to 36,500 nationwide. This figure was presented at the Third National Conference of Women Construction Workers, which took place in Havana in 1980. Another fact to emerge from the conference is that administrators and foreman still prefer to hire men because a man's aptitude for construction work is allegedly higher. This attitude, best noted, goes against every principle governing the making of the new society.

Women constitute 30 percent of the Cuban work force. The distribution of women in different sectors of the economy is as follows:

Category	1974	1978	Increment
Labor	153,453	189,476	36,023
Services	186,924	204,448	17,524
Technical	143,211	216,383	73,172
Management	83,927	125,854	41,927
Executive	28,401	37,702	9,301

Women in Management. The promotion of women to positions of political leadership and national administration is a priority of revolutionary policy.

Although positive changes have been made, the number of women in leadership and adminstrative positions does not reflect the great influx of skilled women into the work force.

In 1980 the percentage of women candidates and elected officials dropped. The percentage has in fact been dropping since 1976, when women represented 13 percent of those running for office and 8 percent of those elected. In 1979 these indices dropped to 10 percent and 7 percent respectively.

FMC president Vilma Espín declared at the FMC's Third Congress: "We believe that false conceptions of and prejudices against women still prevail. We believe that the extra workload the majority of women still face presents an obstacle to their promotion.

"This is to warn and motivate competent organizations to undertake a study which would permit taking the proper measures in the next election.

"The FMC should intensify its ideological work to assure that a greater number of women are elected to responsible positions in Organizations of Popular Power. In many cases women set limits on themselves, and in others, subjective factors dominate the minds of the voters and cause them to choose men, thinking their limitations are fewer. When a woman has the necessary qualifications, she should not be discriminated against."

A 1976 survey by the CTC taken in 211 workplaces around the country revealed that 86 percent of those who responded believed the reason so few women held management positions was because housework limited and burdened them.

Women's participation in prosecutorial and judicial agencies rose to 23 percent of professional and nonprofessional judges in 1978, tripling the percentage of previous years.

Women in Education. Before 1959 education was compulsory, but the number of illiterates was more than a million, the number of semiliterates was also more than a million, and ten thousand teachers were out of work.

In 1953, 23 percent of those persons over ten years of age were illiterate; 71 percent had little or no formal schooling; and not even one percent of Cuban women had ever been to college. The "profession of marriage" was the logical way out.

In 1958-59 there were 717,417 people enrolled in school. In the following year this figure rose to 1,059,119 and by 1979 practically all children between the ages six and twelve were attending school, as were 82 percent of those between thirteen and sixteen years of age. Education is compulsory up to the ninth grade, and plans are being made to extend this up to twelfth grade.

In recent years greater emphasis has been placed on educational quality, with a resulting trend toward devising curricula more relevant to the needs of Cuba's economic and social development.

Between 1978 and 1979 3.5 million people, including children teenagers, and adults, were engaged in formal study, as follows:

Preschool & Primary	1,761,200
Secondary School	645,900
University Preparation	113,400
Technical & Professional Schools	282,100
Adult Education	505,700
University & Graduate School	146,300
Other	35,300

The Cuban educational system, which is completely free, is based on the principle of coupling theory and practice, work and study, as advocated by José Martí and the classical marxists, to develop the student's consciousness that he is a producer of social goods; to lay the groundwork for the elimination of prejudice derived from the division of intellectual and manual labor; to eliminate intellectualism in teaching; and to foster interest in investigating the actual environment.

Once a year, students from the seventh to the twelfth grade spend forty-five days in the countryside working in agriculture. There are also six hundred schools in the countryside where students divide their time between fieldwork and study. These country campuses are very modern and include classrooms, kitchens, dining halls, dormitories, playing fields, and sometimes a swimming pool. They are situated in rural areas where arable land is at their disposal.

Thanks to the FMC's initiative, 162,141 homemakers have passed sixth grade since a campaign was begun in 1975. Another positive outcome of the campaign is that the total number of women who both work and study is 31 percent while the figure for men is only 25 percent. The FMC is also seeking to eliminate the factors that make it difficult for women to study, for instance, by increasing the number of daycare centers.

Cuba offers aid in health and education to many countries of Africa and the Americas. As an example we can cite the 1200 Cuban teachers in Nicaragua, a country where the illiteracy rate is 70 percent. Nicaragua pays nothing for these teachers, who work in rural areas at the primary level for two years. Fifty percent of these teachers are women.

Daycare. Before 1959 there were only 38 daycare centers having a total attendance of 1600 children between the ages of one and six. The centers were run by charities, and the children did not receive adequate educational or medical attention. One after another, politicians used these impermanent institutions to boost their own campaigns; and then once elected they would forget about them.

In 1960 the FMC was put in charge of creating institutions for children that would free women to join the work force, the first step in the struggle for equality.

But it wasn't enough to create schools by adapting the abandoned houses and palaces of the wealthy class that was fleeing the country. Personnel had to be trained quickly to man the schools.

That first year 4000 former domestics were graduated from an intensive training course. In 1969 the first school for teachers of daycare centers was opened as a four-year school.

The Children's Institute, founded in 1971, brought together under its control all daycare centers and institutions dealing with children from birth to five years of age. By 1980 Cuba had 766 daycare centers with space for 70,600 children.

Nevertheless, the existing centers were not enough to satisfy the demand, so the FMC, the Children's Institute, the CTC and Local Power worked intensively together to find short-term solutions.

Children in daycare learn to function collectively and to become responsible for small tasks, such as dressing themselves, setting the table, or caring for garden plants. It is generally accepted that daycare children are better prepared for school and for life in general than children raised by their own mothers, who are often indulgent and possessive.

Mothers in Action for Education. To contribute to the proper education of children and youth the FMC instituted the Mothers in Action for Education Movement. The Movement is comprised of brigades that work in school systems every day to improve attendance levels and reduce tardiness, to help children with their schoolwork, to stimulate sports and recreation, and to do whatever else needs to be done to assure that every school is a model school. They also collaborate to provide study materials and to make sure the children form good social habits. There are 14,954 brigades with a total of 1.4 million members.

Women in Health: Sanitary Brigades. From the very moment of revolutionary triumph women have contributed to the country's health, and it is one of the most expansive tasks anyone has ever been charged with. It all began with first-aid courses. The thousands of federadas who took these courses laid the foundation for today's sanitary brigades.

Today the brigades have more than 56,000 members who make their contributions to various health programs, particularly mother-child programs, resulting in a great deal of support for prenatal care and raising the average number of prenatal consultations so that 98.5 percent of all births now occur in hospitals.

Births, Maternal Homes, Mortality, etc.. Before 1959 more than 60 percent of all births took place at home, and the mortality rate, although no statistics exist, was very high.

At the triumph of the Revolution the Ministry of Public Health created the Department of Women and Children's Medical Attention, which in turn instituted the Maternity Homes. These assure prenatal care for women in isolated areas, but they are built close enough to competent hospitals that the women can also be seen at the hospital.

Each pregnant woman receives approximately nine prenatal checkups, and during the first year of life children also receive approximately nine checkups.

Maternal mortality—because of complications of pregnancy, birth, or postparturition—dropped 62 percent between 1978 and 1959 through the expansion of health facilities that raised the percentage of institutional births to almost 100. This has brought about the complete disappearance of the traditional makeshift midwife.

No other third-world country has reduced, as Cuba did in 1980, its infant mortality rate to 19.4 per thousand. Nicaragua, for instance, has an infant mortality rate of 100.0 per thousand.

The average Cuban lifespan has been lengthened to 70.2 years. The woman's average lifespan is 73.5 years, a fact which, Fidel Castro told the FMC's Third Congress, "because of all the sacrifices and stress women endure, no one can explain."

Free hospital and medical care—even including plastic surgery— has been decisive in lengthening the Cuban lifespan.

The Baby Boom. The last years of Batista's dictatorship were characterized by an extraordinary ferocity. People lived more or less within a constant insurrection. This kept the birth rate very low. Soon after the revolutionary triumph, the birth rate increased so drastically that when it was desired to slow it down, there were difficulties.

Baby boom statistics show that 25 babies were born for every 1000 people in 1959 and 37 for every 1000 in 1965. Thereafter, because of the availability and government support of contraceptives, the rate declines.

Let us call attention also to the increase in births among women under twenty years of age, many of whom are having their second and third children, a medical risk for both mother and child. Many of these babies come into the world fatherless, unwanted, without anything resembling a stable home.

Abortion. One effect of Cuba's underdevelopment in the 1950's was the unavailability of contraceptives. Fertility was controlled by abortion, despite a statute in the Social Defense Code that authorized abortion only "when the continuation of the pregnancy constitutes a grave risk to the mother's health."

Abortion had become a business, the sole business of many gynecologists. Because competency and availability determined prices, the cost was relatively low. Many "tourists" in need of abortions came to Cuba in the 1950's.

From the beginning the Revolution prohibited abortion in unjustified cases, and that explains, in part, the baby boom. In 1962 the Ministry of Public Health sponsored a nationwide investigation of maternal mortality. The findings alerted the public to the fact that at least one third of the maternal deaths were caused by clandestine abortions performed by unqualified persons in inadequate conditions. Work to change this took two directions: more contraceptives were imported, popularized and made available free of charge; and hospital abortions were made easier to get.

This last step became more and more common though the law prohibiting it was never repealed. This was done by giving a more flexible interpretation to that part of the law which read "Interruption of pregnancy is legal when the mother's life is in grave danger." Obviously, one of the greatest dangers to a woman's life is a clandestine abortion. Now, the only prerequisite for abortion is that the woman in question ask for it.

Since 1974 the number of abortions has declined noticeably. It is hoped that this trend will continue, without any need for restrictive measures, on the basis of the socio-economic-cultural development of the country.

The Ministry of Health's chosen solution to the abortion problem is sex education and the popularization of contraceptives.

Sterilization. In 1976 guidelines were established for female sterilization. These stipulate that the patient must be informed of the surgery's irreversible effect, and suggest that both members of the couple should be aware of that fact.

The guidelines, at first very restrictive, loosened until they became today's flexible criteria and left to the discretion of hospital directors. Rarely is a woman younger than twenty-five accepted for sterilization, except in cases where a doctor has prescribed it.

Contraceptives. Before the Revolution it was so hard to find contraceptives that in order to buy diaphragms, for instance, a doctor would have to go in person to the warehouse that imported them. Only a thin upper crust of middle-class professionals used condoms and cocoa butter to provide protection.

Although there is still no well-defined family planning policy, there are programs designed to help regulate the fertility rate.

Today many different kinds of contraceptives are available. Everything from the pill to the IUD is offered free of charge in the country's hospitals.

The condom is not used as much as it ought to be because of sexist influence: it is the woman who is supposed to "take care of herself."

Sex Education. There is clearly a need for a massive sex-education campaign despite all the prejudices which would stand in the way. Today's adolescents have a completely different life style than their parents, although their lack of sex education is almost identical.

The FMC has begun a concrete family education project that includes sex education.

In order to make the project viable, the FMC's Third Congress approved the following aims:

1. To intensify orientation and information through all available means and media to create public awareness of the importance of social, formal, and sex education. To increase the number of informational programs for parents, educators, and the general public.

2. To step up the preparation of materials and the publication of pamphlets, books, and all types of printed matter on the themes here analyzed.

3. To organize training courses for doctors, social workers, medical technicians, nurses, and other personnel with a view to making sex counseling available to couples and families.

When socialist democracy was instituted in 1976 by the constitution of the National Assembly of Popular Power, the FMC brought in a group of specialists who were already preparing materials and giving conferences to professionals and adolescents at different scholastic levels.

The result of their work has been the publication of books for parents and children by recognized sexologists.

The Party, the people's organizations, and other state organizations support the program. It faces no institutional opposition as it does in other countries where organized religion is influential.

Cuba never had sex-education specialists. The first seminar on the subject was held in Havana in 1976. Thirty-six political and people's organizations as well as seven state organizations were represented. The seminar was part of the United Nations Fund for Population Activities (UNFPA) project. Its objectives were to examine the principal characteristics of sex education in Cuba, to acquaint delegates with the same in other countries, and to recommend sex education activities for Cuba.

Women in Sports. The FMC works to promote systematic participation in sports and recreational activities among *Federadas*.

On February 23, 1961, the National Institute of Sports, Physical Education and Recreation (INDER) was legislated into existence on the premise that physical education and recreation are of prime importance to the nation. A year later professional sports were completely abolished.

In 1962 a physical fitness testing program called "Ready to Win" (LPV, *Listos Para Vencer*) was tried all over the island and gained immediate acceptance. The concept behind the program is that man is an integrated being whose physical and mental capacities form one harmonious unit and that the proper view is to see that he is healthy.

For the entire adult population, the Ready to Win tests were something brand-new. Thousands of people, both young and old, passed the tests, which consisted of gymnastics, the long jump, field and track events such as the fifty-meter dash and the one hundred-meter run, rope-climbing, and swimming.

The Ready to Win tests uncovered many exceptionally talented young athletes who had not previously had the chance to show their ability. Since those first years participation in sports has expanded enormously. Now there are playing fields, gymnasiums, and other sports installations all over the country.

These are not casual successes. They are the fruit of the plan implemented by INDER and the Ministry of Education by means of which thousands of primary school teachers qualified to incorporate physical education into their curriculums.

As a result of Cuban sports policy Cuba became the undisputed leader of the Central American Games in Puerto Rico in 1966, and it has held that position ever since. At the Olympics in Mexico in 1968 Cuba took the gold medal in the women's 400-meter relay and in Moscow in 1980 María Caridad Colón won the gold medal in javelin. She was the first Latin American woman to win such a high honor.

The National Scholastic, Workers', University and Military Games, as well as numerous international events in which Cuba participates in search of experience, are of great importance.

At Sports Initiation Schools sports and studies are combined. This is where talented young people take their first steps toward becoming the champions of tomorrow.

Dozens of Cuban sports figures have won important victories. The Cuban women's volleyball team won the Pan-American title on three occasions. It has also won all the Central American and Caribbean events, fifth place at the Montreal Olympics and finally, in 1979, the World Championship. In addition, the team has won over five hundred international games.

In 1976 the FMC initiated "matro-gymnastics," classes which help to create the habits necessary for both good health and better relationships between mothers and children. This program particularly benefits children who are not in daycare centers, since the homemakers come to class with their three- and four-year-old children. In a short time the number of homemakers in basic gymnastics classes has doubled. In the last Workers' Games, 23 percent of the more than one million people who participated were women.

SOME IMPORTANT LAWS

Social Security and Pension. All Cubans have a right to social security. A sick worker can draw up to a year's security benefits, 50 percent of his salary if he stays at home, and 40 percent if he is hospitalized. For sickness caused by occupational health hazards or job-related accidents, an additional 20 percent is paid.

In order to retire a woman should be at least fifty-five years of age and have worked a minimum of fifteen years; a man must be sixty and have worked a minimum of fifteen. Retirement pay is the same for both.

The pension for old-age or physical or mental incapacity is not more than 50 percent of a worker's average annual salary.

Whether she works or not, a woman whose husband dies receives 100 percent of his salary for three months. If the widow does not work, she received 70 percent of his salary after the first three months, 80 percent if there are two dependents, and up to 100 percent if there are three or more.

A working widow receives 25 percent of her late husband's salary after the third month.

The Family Code. The Family Code was proclaimed in 1975 and debated across the nation in all the People's Organizations, such as marriage, divorce, father-child relationships, alimony, adoption, and education. The Code's objectives are:

•To strengthen family bonds of love and affection, mutual help and support.

•To support both legally formalized or officially recognized marriages founded in the absolute equal rights of men and women.

•To contribute to more effective parenting with respect to the protection, guidance, and moral education of children so that they may develop fully in all respects and become worthy citizens of the socialist society.

•To assure that all children, born in or out of wedlock, enjoy equal rights.

The Code establishes that a marriage cannot be formalized unless the bride and the bridegroom are both over eighteen. In exceptional cases, for justifiable reasons, when consent has been legally ascertained, marriage is authorized for a woman of fourteen years or a man of sixteen.

Another article of the Code expresses that partners in a marriage are both responsible for satisfying the needs of the family their union has created, each according to his ability and economic means. Nevertheless, if one partner contributes to family subsistence solely through housework and child care, the other partner should single-handedly provide the family's economic support without this modifying his obligation to cooperate with housework and child care.

The Code also establishes that each partner has the right to work, to practice his profession, to take on new studies, or to improve upon previous studies, and that each partner should support and aid the other in his endeavors. The couple will take pains to organize family life in such a way that these activities do not interfere with compliance with obligations imposed by the Family Code.

Divorce. Divorce can only be obtained by judicial decree, and is authorized when the marriage has lost meaning for both partners and their children.

According to the Code the support of under-age children is the responsibility of both the mother and the father. This holds true regardless of whether on not the children in question are in a parent's custody, care, or keeping or enrolled in an educational establishment.

All children are equal and therefore enjoy equal rights and have the same responsibilities with respect to their parents regardless of the latter's civil status.

The Code defines alimony as everything indispensable to a person's upkeep, such as shelter, clothing, and in the case of minors, whatever else is required for their education, recreation, and development.

Minors can always demand alimony from their parents. Other people with a right to do so can demand alimony when age, incapacity, or lack of economic resources prevent them from supporting themselves. People with a right to demand alimony from each other are spouses; forebears and descendents; the adopted and the adopters; and all siblings regardless of their relation.

The Code of Youth and Children. During its session from the twenty-eighth to the thirtieth of June, 1978, the National Assembly of Popular Power approved the Code of Youth and Children, which establishes the obligations of persons, organizations, and institutions supervising juvenile education as well as the rights and duties of youth.

The Third Article proposes instilling and encouraging the following obligations, among others, in young people:

•The love of truth and justice, the collective spirit, the observance of standards for living in a socialist community, and standards of formal education, moral honesty, and integrity in the treatment of others in public and private life.

•The willingness to fight for the principle of women's equality and mutual cooperation that should govern the relationship of a young couple in marriage, in the fulfillment of their social and domestic obligations, and in caring for and educating their children.

•The feeling of equality, as opposed to discrimination of every kind because of differences in sex, race, color, national origin, or other reason.

A NECESSARY CLARIFICATION

To understand the gains of Cuban women in the last twenty years the reader in any developed country should keep in mind the reality of Cuban women before 1959—the cultural abyss, the underdevelopment, the historic dependency—and the reader will compare the advances of women in developed countries to those of Cuban women only at the risk of detracting from that reality.

It cannot be denied that Cuban women have already won a part of the battle and that they are continuing the struggle from entrenched positions, using the weapons the Revolution has put in their hands, the weapons with which they hope to gain, in an unforeseeable future, their rightful position in society.

The "battle of the sixth-grade"—so-called because every worker in Cuba is obliged to have a sixth-grade education—has been won, and goals have been raised. Workers are now going to classes at night to complete ninth grade, even in remote villages. JØRGEN SCHYTTE

Children in Old Havana get together to do their homework. JØRGEN SCHYTTE

Children start young in a national program of physical education, which is of primary importance to the nation. JØRGEN SCHYTTE

Make room for the new woman—a delighted girl and a gracious old man share the Cuban reality. INGER HOLT-SEELAND

NOTES

1. *Popol Vuh*, sacred text of the Quiche peoples of Guatemala.
2. *Décima*, a poem of ten octosyllabic verses which Cuban peasants improvise to a guitar accompaniment.
3. "among the ancient Maya . . . men and women did not eat together. The women of the house served the men and didn't sit down to eat until the men had finished and gotten up. The same practice was common, until very recently, among Cuban peasants. It can still be observed in places far from cities and roads," Sylvio de la Torre, *Mujer y Sociedad*, Universidad Central de Las Villas, 1965, page 88. In extensive travels through Cuba I have substantiated that the custom is much more alive than de la Torre suggests.
4. *Acopio*, the state organization that collects, buys, and distributes the peasants' farm produce.
5. *Mojito*, a common and popular Cuban mixed drink of Carta Blanca rum, lime, sugar, soda, and ice.
6. Angel María Bétancourt Cueto, pistol in hand, hijacked a Cubana de Aviación passenger plane on March 27, 1966. He ordered the pilot, Fernando Alvarez Perez, to fly to the United States. Alvarez feigned obediance but turned toward Cuba halfway through the flight. As the plane landed, Alvarez told the hijacker they had arrived in Miami, but Betancourt was not fooled; he fired at Alvarez and the guard Edor Reyes, killing them both, and wounding the co-pilot Evans Rosales. Betancourt fled and was apprehended thirteen days later in the Convent of Saint Francis. He was executed on June 15 of the same year.
7. *Le Coubre*: The mysterious explosion of the *Le Coubre*—a French steamship filled with arms Cuba had bought from Belgium—rocked Havana on March 4, 1960. Nearly a hundred people were killed and two hundred others were wounded.

8. More than a thousand armed soldiers, Cuban residents of the United States, disembarked under John F. Kennedy's orders in the Bay of Pigs region. They were defeated by Fidel Castro's troops.

9. The October Crisis came in 1962 when the United States ascertained that missiles capable of carrying nuclear arms were being installed in Cuba. American warships blockaded the island and brought the world to the brink of a third world war.

10. October 6, 1976. On board Cubana de Aviación's plane number CUT-1201 in routine flight between the Barbados, Kingston, and Havana, a bomb exploded, and the plane crashed into the sea. Cuban counterrevolutionaries engineered this bombing in which 73 people died: 57 Cubans, including 24 competitors on their way home from the Central American Fencing Championship; 7 young Guyanese students holding scholarships for study in Cuba; 5 Koreans; and 4 others.

11. Volunteer work for the Committees for the Defense of the Revolution.

12. Popular Power Assembly: Each election district elects one delegate to the Assembly. Periodically, neighbors gather to express their needs, such as the construction of parks, difficulties in the functioning of some service, and so on. If the Assembly approves, the delegate attempts to have the problem solved. He also reports on the status of previous petitions.

13. A privilege authorized for working women so that they don't have to stand in line to buy food at the grocery store.

14. *Coppelia*, an innovative and modern building devoted exclusively to the sale of ice cream. It covers an entire city block and is surrounded by gardens in the Rampa, a favorite meeting place for young people and the most central zone of Havana.

15. Committeee guard. Every *cederista* on every block has guard duty once a month. Women take the first shift from eleven to two in the morning and men take the two to five shift.

16. *Polimita*, a brightly colored snail native to the eastern mountains of Cuba.

17. *Solar*, multiple dwelling units for poor families.

18. The clean-up of Escambray. In the Sierra del Escambray, a mountainous central region of Cuba, groups of armed Cubans sponsored by the United States rose up in 1961 to combat Fidel Castro's Revolution. They were liquidated by the Revolutionary Militias and the People's Army.

19. The textile mill named "Granma's Landing" in the province of Villa Clara, built at a cost of 142 million pesos, will produce 60 million square meters of high-quality fabric a year. It will be the largest textile mill in the country and will employ five thousand people. A similar mill will soon be constructed in Santiago de Cuba.

20. *Quince,* a party for young women when they turn fifteen. Very expensive because of the clothes, dances, music, food and drink, which is usually ostentatious.
21. Las Yaguas, a marginal neighborhood that disappeared at the triumph of the Revolution. The inhabitants were given new dwellings.
22. Beneficencia. A state institution run by nuns where mothers who were generally having financial difficulties would abandon their children.
23. In April of 1980, the events at the Peruvian Embassy in Havana had world-wide repercussions. Approximately 10,600 people took refuge in the embassy and asked to leave Cuba for, principally, the United States.
24. F. Azcuy Alon, *Psicografia y supervivencia de los aborigenes de Cuba,* A Revista Educación publication, Havana, p. 25.
25. Silvio de la Torre, *Mujer y Sociedad,* Universidad Central de las Villas, 1965, p. 133.
26. Leland H. Jenks, *Nuestro Colonia de Cuba,* Madrid, 1929.